C000148500

Tops of the North

Graham Wilson

TOPS OF THE NORTH

Vol I: Three Shire Head to Carlisle

Drawings by Gerry Dale

Millrace

First published in Great Britain in 2008 by
Millrace
2a Leafield Road, Disley
Cheshire SK12 2JF
www.millracebooks.co.uk

Text © 2008 Graham Wilson
Drawings © 2008 Gerry Dale

ISBN: 978-1-902173-26-9

Typeset in Adobe Garamond Pro.
Printed and bound in the United Kingdom
by T J International Ltd, Padstow, Cornwall PL28 8RW

Acknowledgements

Acknowledgements have a habit of following a pattern which thanks everyone, from the chairman to the tea-lady, for everything. This not only runs the genre's gamut from sycophancy to condescension, but also the risk of substantially reducing the world's natural resources. I was therefore curious to discover the origin of the word. To my surprise, it came not necessarily from the Latinate stem that implies a nod of recognition but with equal possibility from the Old English *acknow*, meaning to confess. This, at least in my case, seems more appropriate as I have to admit I am not at all confident that I have recalled all the sources that have, over the years, contributed to this book. A variety of other authors must have ploughed the soil and planted the seeds, both on the ground and in my mind. I can only hope the bibliography goes some way to gaining absolution.

In the more orthodox manner, I would like to thank Tricia, my wife, and John Goodman, who have, in turn, accompanied me on much of this journey, with an especial acknowledgement to the latter for his support on the transport front. A car at each end of a section is a blessing indeed. This also seems an appropriate moment to thank my publishers Millrace, and Viv Cripps in particular, who throughout the past decade have offered advice, encouragement and support far beyond any contractual obligation.

Graham Wilson

Note to Readers

Readers are reminded that although the information in this book is based on the author's own experience, circumstances can change. This is particularly true of hilly countryside, through which the majority of this route passes. It is the individual's responsibility to assess his or her ability to undertake the journey, or any part thereof, in the manner described.

Contents

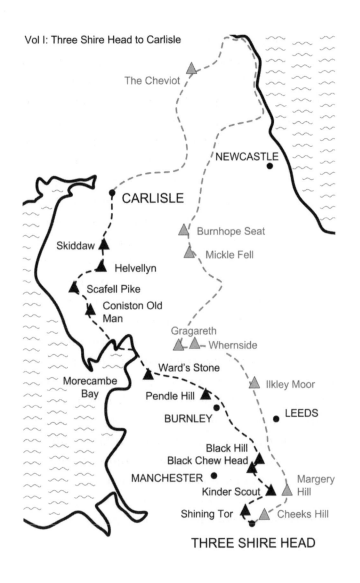

Vol I: Three Shire Head to Carlisle

The Cheviot

NEWCASTLE

CARLISLE

Burnhope Seat

Skiddaw

Mickle Fell

Helvellyn

Scafell Pike

Coniston Old Man

Gragareth

Whernside

Ward's Stone

Morecambe Bay

Ilkley Moor

Pendle Hill

BURNLEY

LEEDS

Black Hill
Black Chew Head

MANCHESTER

Margery Hill

Kinder Scout

Shining Tor

Cheeks Hill

THREE SHIRE HEAD

Welcome to the North: an introduction
The Western Reaches

In the 1950s there was, and as far as I know still is, a traffic sign situated in Central London that implied that THE NORTH lies somewhere at the top of the Edgware Road. In other words, that outside the impenetrable jungle that is St John's Wood, there exists an unknown and somewhat alarming world populated by shadowy figures and dark satanic mills. The inhabitants of the Home Counties, comforted by the knowledge that their forebears had built a series of protective walls and ramparts and struck a deal that any opposition found hard to refuse, rested for the most part content in the bower of their City bonuses and hopes of thermaling house prices.

The more intrepid, however, unable to resist the call of the pipes, would, after travelling the best part of 600 miles and finding themselves on Route 832 to the Misty Isle, be surprised to observe another road sign which curiously appears to announce the same destination. The immediate reaction—that their beloved Scotland (i.e. the said Misty Isle, Edinburgh Castle and the anvil at Gretna Green) had somehow managed to remain an enclave of The South for the benefit of retiring gentlefolk—must have been one of immense satisfaction. Yet in the stilly watches, as they lay awake computing whether a one-and-a-half bedroom flat in Islington could convert to a mediaeval manor with a good slab of Dumfriesshire attached, they might well have pondered where the fabled North actually was.

They would not be alone. Any aspirant creator of the Great Northern Novel hoping to fill that missing panel of the English provincial triptych partially completed by *Sons and Lovers* and *Tess of the D'Urbervilles* must have fingered this particular Gordian knot. And such is its ravelment that to write even a simple guidebook about the area means that the question of the true topographic nature of the North of England cannot be ducked. Of the bounds north, east and west there is little doubt. If, Canute-like, you attempt to fiddle with the oriental or occidental, you are likely to get very wet. As for the northerly border—it's all a matter of crows. Any self-respecting bird-spotters' book will tell you that while *Corvus corone corone*, otherwise known as the carrion crow, is common throughout England, its role is usurped once the Border has been crossed. Here the hooded crow, or *Corvus corone cornix*, holds sway, with a clear sense of where it stands. You can travel north on the A68 and, if tempted to pause at the Border Viewpoint of Carter Bar, you will be quickly aware that you are under scrutiny from the local hoodies, for so they are known, checking out intruders as did the stravaiging Reivers long ago. So, there is little problem with three points of the compass but this is not the case when it comes to the southern collimation. At what moment do travellers from Carlisle or Berwick-upon-Tweed feel that they have reached the point on the A6 or A1 where they have left the North and are entering a land where the primary function of sex is to ease the transportation of coal?

The difficulty is componded by the variety of opinion on offer. No less a body than the Rugby Football Union has decreed, from time immemorial, that the North of England should consist of the counties of Cheshire, Cumberland and Westmorland, Durham, Lancashire, Northumberland and Yorkshire. I suspect, however, that this decision was prompted more by the distribution of Public Boarding Schools than as a result of any thorough demo-geographic investigation. A straw poll among any group of potential border dwellers who yearn for the hills is unanimous—the North starts at a line just south of where they live or were born. Nor does a close examination of the relevant maps help. Much of Derbyshire and a good slab of Lincolnshire lie well above most of Cheshire and, indeed, a fair bit of Lancashire and Yorkshire. Yet neither cut the mustard with the RFU, which lumped them along with Nottinghamshire as a composite county in the Midlands.

As, however, the intention of this book is to record an upland walk and the nature of Northern-ness, there are good reasons for removing Lincs from this particular equation, even if the present rate of global warming does not do it first. For a start, its highest point is only a scratch over 500 feet and its renowned daughter of Grantham was not known for her admiration of those who were employed in such northern pastimes as coalmining and shipbuilding. Derbyshire is a different kettle. In the Peak District, Kinder Scout and Bleaklow rise above the 2,000-foot contour and the Iron Lady's political counterpoint, the Beast of Bolsover, was, in common with his constituents, less than sympathetic to entrepreneurial flummery.

But a decision had to be made if this roundabout was ever going to start and I decided the packhorse bridge at Three Shire Head, where the counties of

Staffordshire, Cheshire and Derbyshire come into collision, would be the most suitable southernmost point. Others will no doubt disagree but I would call as witness the jaggers and their trains who must have felt that here, with the rough moorland and notorious men of Flash behind them, they and their load had entered another and more hospitable land. And from my point of view, when the going gets tough, the North gets going.

Having decided the ground, I could turn my attention to the format. Some years ago, when rounding up the Munros, I travelled to Scotland on a regular basis with a fellow enthusiast. Each evening Ron would spend some time poring over the map, engrossed in the lay of the land and the possible difficulties that might arise if matters got really nasty—a prudent approach in the best tradition of wild country wandering. Eventually, he would meticulously refold the map and deliver his opinion as to whether the morrow was to be a 'one-can' or a 'two-can' day. The cans in question contained beer, for Ron firmly believed that a modest injection of the requisite stimulant at a suitable moment would enhance performance in the field. I have no doubt that many famous military victories were founded on the same principle. He was not an over-indulgent man and regarded two as a sensible limit. There had been talk of a 'three-can' stravaig around what seemed to be the whole of Sutherland, but I had tempered his ambition by pointing out that two shorter walks would later allow more time in the pub.

When assessing the extent and nature of my present task, I quickly realised that this had to be a 'two-can' book. Therefore, what follows is Volume I of a two-part effort and covers the areas to the west, finishing at the Scottish border. Volume II, crossing the more easterly section of the North and returning to Three Shire Head, will, I hope, follow as soon as possible.

So, having decreed the general nature of the format, all that remained was to decide on the particular. The idea was to work out a roughly circular continuous walk that covered most of the high land in northern England. The ground rules were straightforward: I must visit each of the County Tops and keep to the high ground wherever possible. But, as so often happens, the solution of one problem can lead to the creation of another. In this case, when is a County Top not a County Top? Prior to 1974 the matter was relatively straightforward, the only exception being Mickle Fell, which lay on the Westmorland/Durham/Yorkshire border and was, depending on circumstances, claimed or disowned by the surrounding authorities. The others (Black Hill, Cheshire; Kinder Scout, Derbyshire; Coniston Old Man, Lancashire; Scafell Pike, Cumberland; Cheviot, Northumberland) were pretty clear and stood aloof from any potential turf war. Matters might be helped if your route included Helvellyn, Burnhope Seat and Whernside, as well as Mickle Fell, where you would have covered any alternative claim that might be put forward by the relevant counties. Moreover, these anomalies could be fitted comfortably and advantageously into any circular planning.

Post 1974, owing to the reorganisation of local government, matters became more complicated. Cumberland, Westmorland and the Furness district of Lancashire were, for the most part, lumped together in the new county of Cumbria. This meant two of the old Tops disappeared and Lancashire lost its toehold in the Lake District. All the Duchy received in return was Gragareth, a somewhat insignificant bump that previously had remained undisturbed by the hordes thundering around the adjacent Yorkshire Three Peaks. Even the most fervent Lancastrian would have been hard pushed to use Gragareth in any sort of Roses counterclaim against the perceived superiority of the likes of Ingleborough and Whernside and would probably happily disown it in favour of Ward's Stone or Pendle Hill, which at least are free-standing with a substantial drop on all sides. In addition, Black Hill escaped the clutches of the Bishops of Chester who, with an appropriate sense of the temporal, had claimed sovereignty over the neck of land that was the conduit for the valuable cargo of salt from the Cheshire Wiches to the Yorkshire Abbeys. Black Hill, otherwise known as Soldier's Lump, was now the highest point in the West Riding.

The good news was that the new Cheshire high point was Shining Tor, which was conveniently close to, but fortunately north of, Three Shire Head, and that the Mickle Fell dispute had been resolved as it now lay clearly in Durham. The bad news was a mushrooming of a set of sub-counties, many of whom would, if included, have produced a storm of protest from the Wolds. Clearly a further restriction had to be applied if matters were not to get completely out of hand. Not least of the problems was that it would tax the most determined metaphysician to decide whether the Angel of the North or the ego of the average chairman of Newcastle United FC was the more exalted in the municipality of Tyne & Wear. The simple answer was to include all County Tops as listed both before and after 1974, but to have a cut-off point to reflect the fact that the walk is intended as an exploration of the high ground in the region. The point I chose was 350m, the approximate height at Three Shire Head, on the grounds that your ends should be rather more lofty than your beginnings.

The boundary shifts resulted in a further surprise. The highest point in Staffordshire, the aptly named Cheeks Hill, is now further north than the starting place. So a table of Tops would read:

Pre-1974

Cheshire	Black Hill
Cumberland	Scafell Pike
Derbyshire	Kinder Scout
Durham	Burnhope Seat
Lancashire	Coniston Old Man
Northumberland	The Cheviot
Westmorland	Helvellyn
Yorkshire	Mickle Fell

Post-1974

Cheshire	Shining Tor
Cumbria	Scafell Pike
Derbyshire	Kinder Scout
Durham	Mickle Fell
Greater Manchester	Black Chew Head
Lancashire	Gragareth
Northumberland	The Cheviot

Staffordshire	Cheeks Hill
North Yorkshire	Whernside
South Yorkshire	Margery Hill
West Yorkshire	Black Hill

Thus making fourteen separate County Tops in all.

Once these have been established, the route becomes pretty clear and the newcomers and potential anomalies fall conveniently into place. Black Chew Head lies between Kinder and Black Hill. You could, if you wanted, include Pendle Hill and Ward's Stone in your traverse across Lancashire and deem them honorary members of the group. An extensive tour through the Lake District is a *sine qua non* of any such walk as this, so the Old Man and Helvellyn are a delightful bonus rather than an inconvenience. Burnhope Seat and Mickle Fell are, more or less, cheek by jowl and Gragareth can easily be accommodated in an extended tour of the Three Peaks. Black Hill is whatever you wish and if done on the outward leg leaves the Hills of Margery and Cheeks as the final County Tops on the return journey.

Such a combination would *inter alia* encourage you to cross, rather than circumnavigate, Morecambe Bay, visit a large section of Hadrian's Wall and discover the becastled Northumbrian coastline. All in all, by the time you have signed off you will have a fair idea of the place. And I suppose that is why I decided upon it. In one sense I knew the area pretty well. I was born on Merseyside, reared in Durham and spent most of my working life in Cheshire. Much time and energy had been expended in the National Parks of the Peak and Lake District and my formative climbing experiences ranged around Northumberland from Crag Lough to Hen Hole on Cheviot via the crags of Cullernose Point. I must have visited most of the cathedrals and not a few of the pubs. But before total debilitation set in, I was determined to look at the place as a whole, to see it as a continuous stream rather than a series of pools.

So, having decided *where* the North was, I wanted to consider *what* it was. My gut feeling was that the North had a much stronger regional identity than other parts of England. The mass of the Midlands is amorphous and although there is fierce local pride in various pockets, I do not get the impression that those of Gloucester and Cornwall feel they belong to the same South West clan. In my experience, the men of the North come together quite easily and when they have a common cause it seems to matter more to them than it does to most. Whether it is the constriction of definite boundaries or a sense of mutual suffering that has produced this fellow-feeling I am not certain, but I am sure if you asked an average New Zealand All Black which provincial English rugby team he most feared, the answer, given previous encounters, would be the North. But that does not answer the question *what?* It may be unique, but in what way? And, assuming it ever was, is it still?

Of course the stereotype is simple. The North is not the South. Not the South with its purse-mouth vowel sounds and booming boarding school banter. More flat vowels, flat caps and whippets. For such is the stereotype that spawned the likes of Andy Capp and Coronation Street. The belief is well summed up by a quote from Graham Turner's *The North Country*. He interviewed an alderman of Liverpool who advised him to look at the lorries going down the M6 loaded with steel. 'Now that,' he said proudly, 'is the North! Then watch them coming up the road, loaded with dog food—that's the South East!' It was the last word that exposed the fallacy. It was never the South as a whole with whom the Northerners had a quarrel. In fact they probably had much in common with the miners of the Midlands and the fishermen from Cornwall. 'We mackem, you tackem' is a jibe thrown by the inhabitants of Sunderland towards their effete neighbours in Newcastle but the insult could equally apply to those in the South who, so it was believed, have not only rigged the educational system, the elections and redistribution of wealth in their favour, but also selected all representative sporting teams from a blatantly biased viewpoint. A whole new sport, Rugby League, sprang from this latter assumption.

Like all stereotypes, much of the so-called truth was anecdotal myth that supported a preconceived prejudice. Not all of the South was populated by estate agents, dodgy second-hand car salesmen and shiftless individuals who pronounced themselves company executives, any more than all the people of the North used their bath to store coal or kept ferrets down their trousers. Nevertheless, there must have been some common characteristic that produced the Pilgrimage of Grace, the Jarrow marchers and the stance against pit closure in the Thatcher era. There must, at least, have been a collective understanding that the alchemists of the City, then and now, wanted to turn jobs and communities into hedge and private equity funds and that it was right to unite against them.

Even if this difference was once the case, it seems likely that population shifts and cheap imports, with the consequent disappearance of the heavy industries, mean that the bond has been diluted and with each generation it will continue to be so. Like the English language itself, where variations of accent and dialect have been steadily eroded into some form of universal Kwikspeak, so the Thames Estuary will inexorably submerge us all. Perhaps then the real North will re-emerge. The North of this walk. A land that provoked poets and novelists—a shifting mist of gashed crags, black-brown peat and the curlew calling.

— 1 —

Always a little further
Three Shire Head to Marsden

The reason for starting at Three Shire Head was a personal one. Just down the road is the Rose and Crown which, before it began its career as a pub, was the family homestead where my mother's forebears farmed. So, in a sense, it is the soil from which I sprang and, if not literally, it was, at least, a metaphorical soil fertilised by a particular form of creative fiction. One of my earliest memories is of my mother telling me stories concerning her mother and her mother before her whose ambition was to shake off that soil and seek out the bright lights, in this case the relatively dubious brilliance of Macclesfield. I realised somewhat later in life that the added and most interesting detail probably owed as much to the latest offering at the local cinema as it did to accurate historical record, but I was held in thrall by the doings of the rogues of Flash and gentlemen wearing silk shirts who populated a landscape that was part Wuthering Heights, part southern state of Georgia.

And so, on the roundabout that is not only one life but the intertwining of many, I happened to return to my great-grandmother's Promised Land. First, after our Teutonic cousins set about eliminating a large portion of Merseyside and I had been hauled from the remains of what had turned out to be a rather temporary abode. Second, when I took up employment in the town for thirty-odd years. To sort out the first, i.e. the housing problem, I was sent to my great aunt, addressed variously as Auntie Con or Auntie Em, depending on which part of the family you were a scion of. I don't know whether this sort of nominal duplication is unusual but it seemed to be endemic in my family. I had a second cousin of the variously removed variety who used to refer, with some enthusiasm, to his mysterious aunt and her doings and it wasn't until much later that I realised that he had been talking about a person whom I had known intimately but by an entirely different name. Even my father and my uncle, his brother, were double-barrelled, so to speak. I am not sure if there was any logic behind this apparent duplicity but it might explain the family interest in the said 'creative fiction'.

The detail of my evacuation is rather blurred. A very large thatched building passed on our daily walks, a silver fox that breathed ominously from the dressing room table at night but was completely mute during the day, a pear orchard whose fruit defied not only teeth but even a determinedly driven six-inch nail. One part of this extended family was Aunt Flo, who had a budgie called Budgie and a husband called Will. The latter was probably too old for regular employment but would regale me with tales of how he had 'dropped on' a variety of items during his daily travels. I can't really remember the purpose or method involved in this daily swoop, though I do recall a length of drainpipe that was held in some reverence. But there is no doubt that the event that sticks most clearly in my mind was a picnic at what I later discovered was Three Shire Head. It's quite a long way from Macclesfield and how we got there I have little idea. Buses, pushchairs and lots of women seemed to feature. I threw a fairly large stone off the bridge which appeared to cause quite a stir.

So, from a personal view, the meeting of three shires seemed a reasonably apt place to start. Yet it stands on its own two feet as a fit and proper place for anyone who wishes to begin a journey. This is a genuine meeting of the ways. Less an accidental bumping together of paths than a logical, if not singular, point of coincidence. Stages of many journeys have stopped and started here. Horses were watered, news was gathered, money changed hands. 'Flash', a seventeenth-century term for counterfeit money, was not unconnected with the eponymous village up the road as the locals would gather at the bridge on the safe assumption that law-enforcing officers of all three counties would not appear simultaneously. Hopping from one extra-jurisdictional ground to another must have been one of their various skills. Anyway, that was my mother's story. Matters, of course, have taken a very different turn. Flash has recently been confirmed as the highest village in Britain and no doubt this loftiness is reflected in the current standard of moral integrity.

But there are no rules that cannot be broken and as the whole route is a continuum, you can start and finish wherever you please. The pragmatic might choose the Cat and Fiddle, which is the highest coaching inn in England. It was built by a local banker to cash in on the newfangled craze for foreign travel (in this case Macc to Buxton) and can be reached from my chosen starting place by a bridleway that stretches from the A54 to finish at the pub's front door. The bridleway, in turn, can be reached from Three Shire Head via the burgeoning Dane and a ventilation shaft which assisted the Duke of Devonshire (albeit vicariously) to mine the coal that fired the lime that made the mortar that supported the bricks that built the mills

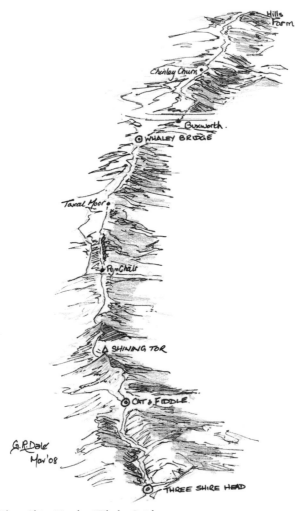

Hills
Farm

Chinley Churn

Buxworth

WHALEY BRIDGE

Taxal Moor

Pym Chair

△ SHINING TOR

CAT & FIDDLE

G. R. Dale
Nov '08

THREE SHIRE HEAD

Three Shire Head to Whaley Bridge

that made the money that founded the wealth of the few—and the misery of the many.

After the Cat and Fiddle, the first of our County Tops is in sight. Shining Tor is not as aloof as Shutlingsloe, the summit that catches the eye in this part of the world, but it is a decent enough hill. For a start, it is the launch pad of a continuous ridge that flows over Cat Tor, Pym Chair, Windgather and Taxal Edge to cross the B5470 at Gap House. From here field paths lead down to and past Toddbrook Reservoir and into Whaley Bridge.

As you can see from this account of the first section of the journey, it is not my intention to write a stile by stile saga of the route. I hope to produce a recollection of a journey rather than a recipe book. As it is, virtually all of the route appears in a variety of other publications which, for the benefit of those who want such things, are listed in the Appendix. Post-Wainwright and Tom Stephenson's Pennine adventure (did either man ever contemplate what he might have started?), 'Ways' have proliferated and paths that were once cherished entrances into solitude and adventure are now stone-paved escalators. I do not wish to add to Satnav Land. With open access to all non-cultivated land which, in turn, is connected by a cats-cradle of rights of way, you can and arguably should go where you like, rather than where others suggest. If you think this route is an interesting one, then, prompted by Gerry Dale's illuminating drawings, follow it by all means. If not, plan your own!

Careful examination of the map shows that you can wriggle out of Whaley by a series of footpaths to the Navigation Inn at Buxworth. More circuitously, you can follow the canal to the same place. From here, with a little planning, you work your way up to and around Chinley Churn before crossing the A624 just above Hills Farm. You are now really in the black stuff and once Brown Knoll has been circumnavigated you reach the meeting of the ways at Edale Cross. If you haven't done so before, it would be as well to take stock and plan the logistics of getting from this point to Marsden. In fact, it would probably be better to have sorted all this out before you left Three Shire Head. The essential problem is that there is only one resting place between Whaley Bridge and Marsden and that is the Youth Hostel at Crowden.

The question is, whether you get your head down and do the whole journey from Three Shire Head in one fell swoop or try to divide it into two manageable parts. Whaley Bridge to Crowden is perfectly feasible by joining the Pennine Way and taking in

Derbyshire's highest point on Kinder. This will also enable you to keep your height over Mill Hill and across Bleaklow before descending to Crowden. The alternative is to drop down to Edale, spend the night there and with fresh legs regain the Kinder plateau. If not of lemming disposition and you want to avoid Edale's version of the Calvary Stampede, then this is done best by ascending Ringing Roger rather than Grindsbrook Clough. In fact, if energy levels are sufficiently boosted, you could eschew most of *the* Way by dropping down to the Snake Pass and regaining the Bleaklow plateau which is crossed directly to Crowden via Torside Clough and the gap between Torside and Woodhead reservoirs. I would prefer the latter, with a spot of lunch at the Snake Inn. But unless you can summon a support party to whisk you to and fro at predetermined road crossings, you will have to take your choice one way or another and, as the adage has it, one way and another, you will probably pay for it.

As you stroll unhindered apart from several posses of Pennpushers, it is worth considering how history has allowed this unimpeded progress. The concerted struggle to allow access really began at the beginning of the last century and continued, with a greater or lesser degree of success, over the following hundred

The Hollins

Crowden Y.H.

Bleaklow Head

Alport Low

Snake Road

Mill Hill

Kinder Downfall

△ CROWDEN HEAD

Ringing Roger

Edale Cross

EDALE

Hills Farm

Chinley Church

G.R.Dale Mar '08

Buxworth

◎ WHALEY BRIDGE

Whaley Bridge to Crowden

years. The most striking single attempt to assert the rights of the common man was the Mass Trespass that came about in 1932. The facts that surround an event that shook the world of rambler and landowner alike are well documented, but the detail deserves some consideration. On Sunday 24th April, 500 ramblers, led and inspired by Benny Rothman, set out from Hayfield to trespass across the Kinder Plateau and meet up with a like-minded group from Sheffield. They had made no secret of their intentions and the landowners rallied a force of keepers and policemen, led by the Deputy Chief Constable, to keep them at bay. Such were their numbers and solidarity that the forces of law and order could do nothing to stop them and the mission was successfully completed.

Once the crowd, whose behaviour had been exemplary, closing gates behind them, leaving no litter and taking every step to avoid physical confrontation, had dispersed, the police struck. They arrested six of the ringleaders and charged them with unlawful assembly and breach of the peace. They were committed to Derby Assize, where a jury consisting of two Brigadier-Generals, three Colonels, two Majors, three Captains and two Aldermen convicted five of the six to a term of imprisonment. It was widely known that some of the defendants were members of various left-wing organisations. The judge, recognising the difficulty, inflamed the situation, unwittingly or otherwise, by instructing the jury that it must ignore any political beliefs that the defendants might hold. Nor were matters improved when he stressed the fact that three of the defendants, Rothman, Nussbaum and Clyne, had strange sounding (i.e. Jewish) names, should also not influence the jury's decision.

To discuss the legal niceties as to whether they were guilty beyond 'all reasonable doubt' is now rather beside the point. What was and remains the point was that the sentences handed out had enormous consequences. With the exception of one, all were imprisoned for a combined total of fourteen months. The general public would probably have ignored the affair if the sentences had been suspended or the accused had been fined, but for a man to be regarded in the same light as a thief or a murderer because he chose to go for a stroll on a Sunday afternoon stirred the nation's conscience and what previously had been a local difference now became a matter of national concern. Memories of the Great War were still very much alive and the countryside that the ramblers were accused of violating was the very same for which their fellow men had laid down their lives.

Once the can was opened, the worms crawled out.

Much of the land in question was originally common land and therefore traditionally open to all. As it was unfit for grazing sheep, there was a sense of live and let live, at least as far as interaction between humans was concerned. The grouse were not so lucky. Then the various Enclosure Acts caused a significant change. They meant that the landowners could legally claim and fence in what they were entitled to or, as often happened, illegally could lay their hands on. Playing safe, they duly did. But, in the beginning, even that did not cause any real friction. The traditional method of grouse shooting was 'over dogs'. i.e. the dogs flushed out the birds and the humans took a pot at them as they tried to escape (birds that is, not dogs). You had to be fit and persevering to take up this pastime, so relatively few did. Matters changed with the introduction of 'driving', and the size of the kill measured the success of the shoot. The intrepid hunters stood behind their butts with as much ordnance and munition as their keepers could carry. The birds were driven back and forth across the line, until, exhausted by continual hounding, they fell, at times literally, into the sportsman's lap. Carnage was all. Amid, no doubt, much back-slapping a record was established when 1,070 fell to the single gun of Lord Walsingham in a day.

As all this took place behind the alfresco equivalent of closed doors, it had done little to disturb the sensibilities of a nation that had died to ensure its continuance. The greater provocation was the use of the police to safeguard particular rather than general interest. As with the miners' strike in the last part of the last century, the use of force by a supposed impartial agency to support the selfish concerns of the establishment was seen by many as unjust. As simple trespass to land has not ever been a criminal offence, the police had no jurisdiction to restrict access to the Derbyshire moors. The worm had not only got out of the can but had started to turn. It was inevitable that all matters of private ownership would come under scrutiny.

Nevertheless, matters still dragged on. Partly because when the Labour Party seized power on behalf of the people, there were greater injustices to resolve. Partly because the pro-access opinion was absolutely divided as to the better way forward, whether it be action or negotiation. As a result, it was easy enough for the landowners to divide and rule and encourage procrastination. The Peak District and Northern Counties Footpath Preservation Society was totally opposed to the idea of the Mass Trespass and firmly believed that the preservation of rights of way should be pursued in a strictly legal manner. This was not altogether a surprise, as one of the vice-presidents of the society was James Watt, the man who actually owned the summit plateau of Kinder Scout. So the landowners and their professional lackeys infiltrated and influenced the decisions of the compromisers and branded the activists communists, or worse.

Almost seventy years later, the right to roam freely was legally granted, but old wounds still ached. In 2002 Benny Rothman died and the newsletter of The Peak and Northern (as it now is) debated the possibility of erecting a signpost, preferably on Kinder, as a memorial to, as *The Guardian* dubbed him, 'the Patron Saint of the British Outdoor Community'. The newsletter also reported sadly that a decision had not yet been reached, as it was still possible 'to detect an undercurrent of opposition, antagonism caused by profound differences in approach to the solving of problems of access'.

Next day you will leave the Hostel and proceed up the depression caused by Crowden Brook. If, on your way up, you are passed by some walkers lolloping their way down, they are more than likely attempting the Marsden–Edale, a classic 'Big Walk' of around twenty-five miles. This has for long been a test piece for the serious (though some may disagree with that choice of epithet) Peak District walker. Its longevity and, no doubt, conception arose because it started and finished at railway stations that are easily accessible from Manchester. You leave the metropolis from Victoria and return to Victoria. It is, without doubt, an odyssey that is more easily accomplished by public transport than car. Given a sympathetic timetable, the averagely good fell runner could leave after an earlyish breakfast, complete the course and be home for a latish lunch.

It is thought that Ross Evans was the first man to complete the course in a single journey. But the concept was formed, as were many similar, by Cecil Dawson, a successful Manchester cotton merchant. Known throughout the rambling community as The Colonel, he was at the centre of many exploits, ranging from a successful attempt on the Lake District's fell-walking record to developing a number of ruses to escape the local keepers' wrath. Others were quick to follow. Alf Bridge, a rock climber as well as a strong walker, one weekend left Greenfield at midday Saturday, completed a climb on Laddow, Stanage, Cratcliffe Tor and Castle Naze (get out the map!) before catching the last train home to be at work on Monday morning. Finally, in 1953, to mark the Coronation, 'Larry' Lambe and John Sumner did a complete horseshoe around the Dark Peak from Hen Cloud on the Roaches to Matlock. These and many other feats are fully covered in Byne and Sutton's *High Peak*, an outstanding account of the story of walking and climbing in the Peak District. The art that Dawson and his fellows perpetrated was known as bogtrotting and consisted of covering vast tracts of land in a half-running, half-walking action that prevented the body-weight sinking into the Derbyshire peat. An art sadly neglected by today's Pennine Wayers who, laden with the kitchen sink, carve, in perpetuity, their own way to Kirk Yetholm.

Great distances were covered and challenges unearthed. For many, the circuit of the Derwent Watershed, starting and finishing at Yorkshire Bridge, was the zenith, but for the few it was a case of farther and further. Yet distance is but one way of measuring achievement. The other is time taken and once again the Marsden–Edale became the centre of attention. As with the four-minute mile, a specific and memorable time is always a tempting target. For the bogtrotting world, it was the four-hour Marsden.

Those readers used to easing around a half-marathon in an hour and a bit might think it not much of a challenge but would do well to factor into their assessment the conditions underfoot, around

3,000 feet of ascent and descent, and the weather. The wind tends to blow a little more fiercely on Kinder than on the sunny side of Regent Street. But all challenges are there to be conquered and it was eventually accomplished by Vin Skelton. Others, such as Phil Altman, were not so successful. He died on Bleaklow during his attempt.

It is interesting to speculate what prompted this orgy of self-flagellation. Man has always responded to the chase and the dogged determination to outstay rather than outpace a faster prey must have been an essential ingredient in the genetic soup. Those who chased in packs eventually turned their attention to football, while those who were less attuned to the hurly-burly of team play found their solace in the loneliness of long distance running. Cross-country has always featured in the activities of public boarding schools. Sedbergh's Wilson Run is the oldest continuously-held organised athletic event in England and therefore quite possibly the world. Variations were the paper chase and Hares and Hounds, where the running was given some direction and reasoning process which, I suppose, has now morphed into the sport of Orienteering. The countryman has for long followed breeds of dog in pursuit of the more or less edible. But all these activities had attracted only a relatively small number, usually, of those who had time and money on their hands. The tram routes from Manchester and Sheffield changed all that. Suddenly the Peak District was available for all and to camp at Chew Piece and set out to spend a weekend in the fresh air and wrestle with the rock and the bog must have been to thousands the fulfilment of a scarcely imaginable dream.

This conjecture may have taken you some way up towards Laddow Rocks and at a suitable point you will have to leave the Pennine turnpike to reach the summit of Black Chew Head, the highest point in Greater Manchester. As you peer down at the South Lancs conurbation, you will realise at once that you have left the comforts of leafy Cheshire and the teashops of Derbyshire. This is what remains of Millopolis, whose inmates disgorged every Saturday afternoon, leaving the workplace to queue with patience and expectation at the gates of their particular place of worship. Names like North End, Rovers, Wanderers lie not only at your feet but forever engraved on the FA Cup. And this illustrious pediment is supported by such caryatids as Rochdale, Oldham, Bury and the never-to-be-forgotten Accrington Stanley. The nature of football and the North is inextricably linked.

Even in these Murdoch-smeared times, the northern sides hold sway, their hegemony threatened only by the fuel-injected clubs of London's Baby Bentleyland. Football is the one product of the Industrial Revolution that so far has withstood the second Harrowing of the North. Perhaps, after all, when it came to football of whatsoever code, the RFU knew what it was about when it drew the line where it did. The best of Derbyshire and Lincolnshire, like small boys, can only try to climb onto the fence in the hope of catching a glimpse of the action.

The Way is rejoined and continued to Black Hill, once Cheshire's finest, now the highest point in West Yorkshire. That particular beaten trail swings westerly along Standedge and its own personal bridge over the M62. We take the alternative to Marsden, quietly slipping into Yorkshire by the now demolished Isle of Skye Inn and Wassenden reservoirs. But the view that you have just left is where you will have to go. After that, the next time you reach another county will be when you've trodden the waters of Morecambe Bay.

— 2 —

Trains and boats and plains
Marsden to Burnley

Marsden lies in a narrowing valley that separates the Peak District from the Pennine hills and moors that, in turn, divide the western counties of Lancashire and Cumbria from Yorkshire and Durham in the east. Threading its way through this channel is a twine of car, train and barge, suggesting that the town stands astride one of the occasional gaps which allows the traveller to squeeze through this hilly countryside at something approaching sea level. But this is misleading. The road might climb over Marsden's western rampart of Standedge but the rail and canal had to burrow its way through the tons of peat-covered rock.

The canal came first. The Huddersfield Narrow, as it is appropriately known, was built in 1794 but such were the problems presented by the intervening obstructions, that the tunnel was not opened until 1811. The constructors, starting from each end, met a series of difficulties and were forced to call in Thomas Telford to advise. He discovered that the way things were going they might end up with two tunnels,

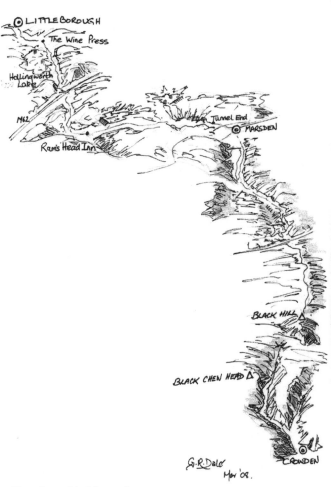

Crowden to Littleborough

instead of one meeting in the middle. To save further time and expense, the canal through the tunnel had to be constructed without a towpath. The bargees, denied their usual horsepower, were forced to 'leg' their vessels through the intervening three-and-a-quarter miles by lying on their backs and indulging the art of horizontal upsidedown walking.

The railway followed some fifty years later and, as steam was somewhat more effective than leg power, soon put the canal under commercial pressure. To add insult to injury, the rail companies made their job considerably easier (and cheaper) by using the waterway to shift their excavated rubbish. In 1894, a second double-track tunnel was built and gradually the canal fell into disuse and eventually closed altogether. But the circle has come round and among the leisure activities that are demanded, boating has become popular. Restoration has been taking place and you can now take a guided trip in a glass-roofed boat.

Our route follows rail and canal until it reaches the aptly if somewhat prosaically named Tunnel End, the main feature of which is a pleasant pub called, not surprisingly, the Tunnel End. Follow the road beside the river until you can join the packhorse route which, after crossing Close Gate Bridge and a short steep pull up Willykay Clough, climbs gently onto the moor. At various points on this journey through the North, my route follows these old routes and you will begin to understand the problems of the jaggers at first hand as they tried to transport fresh salmon from Workington to London or guard valuable cargoes of salt from local marauders. The Peak District must have been the Clapham Junction of its time and I would recommend *Peakland Roads and Trackways* by A E and E M Dodd if you want a closer understanding of the nature of the venture. One by-product of a long inter-regional walk is that the various localities have their own peculiarities and tales to tell, many of which are now permanently recorded by resident historians. It is often worth seeking them out to enrich the experience that you are undertaking— always assuming you can find a bookshop that does not deal exclusively with boy wizards, celebrity cook books or the weighty autobiographies of twenty-two year-old footballers.

But, back on track, you head for the A640 and the A672 before reaching the Ram's Head Inn. En route you will cross the Pennine Way and it will be a long time before you reach any part of it again. You may not be sorry to see it go and even feel a sense of smugness with the superiority of your own path, foot-carved by local craftsmen, rather than bulldozed by twentieth-century technology. On the other hand, you are forced to leave go of the safety-blanket of exhaustively detailed guidebooks with explicit directions on the best way to open gates and climb stiles. You will just have to make do with the Ordnance Survey and a compass. At least you will no longer have to worry about tripping over signs warning against the inexperienced leaving the recognised track unless accompanied by someone in possession of a Mountain Leadership Certificate. Littleborough lies a little north of west in more or less a straight line (unless, of course, you have stayed too long in the Ram's Head) and the route threads its downward path through a posy of reservoirs before climbing once more onto the moorland plateau, then dropping down yet again to its final destination.

At one point, a latter-day Rip Van Winkle might be puzzled as he becomes aware of a sound that resembles a cross between a hum and a roar, but he will probably ignore it in his desire to reach the watershed and see what is on the other side. It is one advantage in walking across the grain, as it were, that you are always likely to chance upon a surprise view. The Victorian tourist guides specialised in such moments and the visitors even carried small mirrors to the approved 'station' and by turning their back to the view and manipulating the reflection over one shoulder, allowed the vista to be the more effectively cropped. It had, they hoped, the same revelatory romance as the sudden parting of the mist. The latter, of course, was the more effective, but rather harder to arrange. But the frame to your particular view is a rather elegantly arched road bridge and that the humroaring, previously heard, was neither an exceedingly large swarm of bees nor the sea pouring into a rock cove, but the M62. More threading takes place through the arches and around the square of the cricket club before the road is reached and Hollingworth Lake is passed on your way to the train station.

If you were to walk this section of the route as a separate journey, you might, through the expedience of placing your car on the forecourt of Littleborough Cricket & Rugby Club and leaving your companion's at the start of your journey, be tempted to avoid the said tarmac. You might even feel that such a course makes life more convenient to arrange. If so, a word of warning. The entrance to the club has not a particularly conspicuous gate, yet the gate has, on closer inspection, a particularly conspicuous padlock. If you get on the wrong side of this padlock and are in the company of a man whose car is in Marsden and has an important evening engagement in Cheshire, matters can be rather awkward. Unless your normal mode of transport is an all-terrain six-wheeled vehicle, the only other possibility is abject apologies and offers of a contribution to club funds.

The modern map bears a legend which accompanies this chain of rights of way and states that it is a 'Station to Station Walk'. As already implied, many parts of the North can be joined in this way and, apart from Littleborough, there are stations at Burnley, Clitheroe, Carnforth and Arnside that can be used to break the route up into manageable parts served by regular public transport. In fact it is only the section through the Forest of Bowland that is isolated from the rail system and even there, with an early start and careful scrutiny of local bus timetables, access is just possible without the need for a car or fear of incurring the wrath of the locals.

If, in fact, you have to spend some time in the fastness of Littleborough C&RF Club car-park, you might eventually consider the ironic circularity of your present position *vis à vis* the transport structure that you have just walked over, under and on. The packhorse was overtaken by the barge with its greater cargo capacity. This in turn had to bend the knee to the train which was quicker and could travel uphill. And when the human race finally decided that walking more than twenty yards was an unreasonable waste of human resources, and was unable to travel to the seaside without the littoral equivalent of an over-equipped garden shed, the car became king. If, as in this case, something incurable happens to your particular transport of delight, despite your most eager protestations and wafting of ten pound notes, the pelican in the wilderness has no sensible alternative but to return to and by the ways of his ancestors.

But let us hope that you are made of sterner stuff, or at least have learnt your lesson and are determined to stride on to journey's end. For 'Station to Station' can only mean what it says. One of the perceived drawbacks to train travel is that you could have to hang around for a connection. If so, Littleborough is worth a visit. Like so many places in its position, it has the feel of a market town partially engulfed by the unstemmed tide of the Industrial Revolution. The square bears witness to the former, ribbon development to the latter. It has a church, the usual accomplishment of pubs and a good new and secondhand bookshop. In fact, it is well worth missing the odd connection.

The orthodox route to the station turns right just

before the Wine Press, a sort of pub-cum-restaurant, and enters the town via Clegg's Wood. However, it is possible, for those in a hurry, to miss the town centre by turning left after the p-c-r, then immediately right down a lane and a series of paths that lead over the canal and under the railway to the A58 and the Sun. The continuation path heads up the stream and lands you on the other side of town at Shore and the King William IV.

The last sentence seems to suggest that the route is perfectly straightfoward but, I fear, the OS has an Achilles heel in that any of its maps may, almost immediately, become out of date. In open moors and hillside any change will have little consequence, but in any conurbation, houses can spring like mushrooms or, perhaps more appropriately, leylandii. On the hill, if you set off in roughly the right direction, you can compensate for any original error of judgement with relative ease. This is not true of the modern housing estate. One false move and you can find yourself in a labyrinth of acacia avenues, enclosed between looming cliffs of mock Tudor fascia and Victorian gig lamps. Intent on guarding their territory, wolves, bears and lynx are as nothing to the dreaded Yorkie as you attempt to escape the cul-de-sac from Hell. The previous scorn heaped on route markers and certificated mountain guides seems hollow and you grasp with gratitude the Right of Way fingerpost when it hoves into view. Even then matters are not always what they seem. There's no NIMBY like the converted and you may find, as I did, that the post has been deliberately twisted to a different direction from the required one, with the intention of dumping you back on the main road where you supposedly belong. It is important to remember, at this moment, that the compass doesn't lie.

Whether you linger in or bypass Littleborough, you must make your way to the King Bill, where a convenient and correctly placed signpost indicates the bridleway to Higher Shore and beyond. If you are intending to cover the twenty plus miles between Marsden and Burnley in one journey, it is probably advisable to time lunch for this hostelry. You will not pass another.

When the high point of the path is reached, you can see your next objective, the moors of Brown Wardle and its satellites on the skyline. Below and to the left is Watergrove reservoir, a large watery expanse that has drowned the village of that name. It is possible to keep some of the height that you have just gained by cutting across the corner. But the way is not obvious and the easier alternative is to keep to the bridleway until you can join the Rossendale Way by climbing the hillside to a point between Brown Wardle and Middle Hill.

Beneath and to the south-west lies Whitworth, former home to the Taylors, an extended family of bonesetters and doctors who practised their art in the eighteenth and nineteenth centuries. By origin, the family were farriers and blacksmiths and it is said that the contents of their surgical bags attested to their former occupation. Indeed, Dr John was in the habit of abandoning a human patient mid treatment if a caller presented a horse that required help. Nevertheless, they enjoyed a remarkable reputation and patients of all classes would travel from every quarter of Britain for treatment. One of those abandoned for the more important horse was no less a personage than the Bishop of Durham. Nor was this visit the pinnacle of the family's hobnobbery. There seems reasonable evidence to suppose the doctors were summoned to minister to various members of the House of Hanover.

The fact that the Taylors of Whitworth were held in such universal esteem is quite an achievement. This was the age of quacks and charlatans and the public were understandably suspicious of their curious medical potions and dubious surgical practices. It

BURNLEY

Leeds
Liverpool
Canal.

Towneley Hall

△ THIEVELEY PIKE

A681

G.R.Dale
Mar'08

HADES
HILL
△

△ MIDDLE HILL

BROWN WARDLE
HILL △

Watergrove
Reservoir

King William IV

LITTLEBOROUGH

Littleborough to Burnley

was estimated that someone entering hospital had as little chance of surviving as did the wounded on the fields of Waterloo and doctors were in the habit of hiring bands to play in the street outside their surgeries in the hope that the noise would drown the screams within. But the Taylors specialised in bonesetting, attempting to cure deformation that had either occurred at birth or through untreated injuries. Their manipulative skills in the days before X-rays must have been of a high order for no less a figure than R Dacre Fox FRCS, Surgeon to the Southern Manchester Hospital and Chief Medical Officer to a number of respected institutions, discussed their methods in an article which appeared in *The Lancet*. This was in effect an abstract of a paper he delivered to the British Medical Council in which he approves of the Whitworth methods and urges his fellow practitioners to direct their attention towards them. The 'method' spread across the world and may well have been instrumental in setting up the renowned Mayo Clinic in Minnesota.

The most authenticated account of the treatment is contained in a memoir dictated to his sister by Archibald Campbell Tait who, with his brother, Ilay Campbell (Camie) Tait, and accompanied by the family nurse, was sent from Edinburgh to

Whitworth. This was no casual visit. The trip started at Leith and landed at Hull, before proceeding to the boys' sister in Chesterfield who, in turn, despatched them, by post, to their final destination.

Archie's legs had been doubled inwards at birth and Camie had suffered paralysis in one of his as a baby. Such was the severity of their disability that they had to remain in Lancashire for some time. Day and night, the boys had to wear boots made of tin while their limbs were returned to their proper function by the use of a 'continual gentle force, the force that comes from gentle pressure'. The continuous pain can only be imagined. But such was the success of the treatment that Camie was passed physically fit to enlist in the navy and Archie became Headmaster of Rugby and, in 1868, Archbishop of Canterbury. An interesting aside is Archie's account of the Red Lion, the local pub where long-stay patients were put up. The boys, unable to follow normal childhood pursuits, spent much of their time in the taproom which was 'full of interest to us'. Probably an unusual formative experience for a future Primate of England.

The Taylors were noted for their interest in foxhunting and cockfighting, but whether their enthusiasm spread to the sport of shin kicking is not recorded. As you pass over Hades Hill and across the mouth of Foul Clough, you cannot but help consider the aptness of the local nomenclature, for these moors housed a pocket of illegal practices, ranging from forgery of bank notes (a crime allegedly perpetrated by members of the Manchester Police) to 'hush-houses' which brewed and sold illicit beer. But the most common breach of the peace was a variety of blood sports, in particular contests of shin kicking. The chief exponents were miners from Oldham, Bacup and Ashton, who challenged the quarrymen from the district around Whitworth. Both parties were no doubt hardened to the task by their daily labours. Apart from a pair of heavy clogs, the contestants competed naked, presumably to offer less grip and prevent illegal padding being hidden under their clothing. The rules appear straightforward: you kicked your opponent until he fell over. Two falls and you won. Any dispute was referred to the umpire, known as a 'stickler'. These were bloody conflicts, often resulting in serious, sometimes fatal injuries. It was little wonder the Taylors set up shop where they did.

The 'sport' still continues and now appears to centre in the Gloucester district but has been gentrified to such an extent that there exists an official organisation that goes under the not inappropriate acronym of

SKAB. As it has moved to the South, the contestants chose to wear jeans, the legs of which were stuffed with straw. Not that the North has avoided a similar dilution of spirit. Shin kicking girlified into clog dancing, the forerunner of tap, and from there it was but a step to the song-and-dance routines so beloved of show biz. If, as you make your way, you find that it is pouring down, you might console youself with the thought that, without the existence of these moors, there would be no such immortal moments of cinema as 'Singin' in the Rain'.

As we are in the process of name-dropping, we might as well mention Lord Byron, poet, freedom fighter and long distance swimmer. He inherited, among other things, the Manor of Rochdale which contained a slab of the land you have been walking across for the past hour or so. With it he inherited a legal wrangle with Simon Dearden, who claimed he had rights to the local coal mining. Byron, whom it might be said was leading a complicated life, decided to cut the Gordian Knot and his losses. He sold the property to the Deardens, retreating to Greece in the hope of improving his all-comers record for swimming the Hellespont.

So, as long—while considering the relative merits of 'Childe Harold' and the works of Gene

Kelly—you don't slip off down the Calder Way, the approved route will take you to your next objective, the high point on that part of the A681 which runs between Bacup and Todmorden. In between the aforementioned musings, you may have noticed that the moorland in these parts has a rather secondhand, not to say distressed, appearance. While this may be fashionable in rustic garden furniture, it is not regarded as the *dernier cri* when it comes to the great outdoors. In fact, as *cris* go, it occupies a lowly point on the scale of things. A number of Deardens and cronies had pillaged the area for a variety of sedimentary deposits before dumping what they did not need on wherever was closest at hand. Future generations did not improve matters.Nature is doing its best to heal the wounds.

Yet these moors may well have the last laugh. They are the true watershed of the Pennines in these parts and could have formed the proper course for any official Way. The imposter you can see to the east, striding towards the monumental folly that crowns Stoodley Pike, is slowly being covered with plastic matting and excavated by vibram. So, when the industrial landscape seeps away like the outgoing tide, it might leave a pristine foreshore, and the villages that were Bacup, Wardle and, perhaps, even Watergrove may reappear and men with horses might call at the door of another Taylor, farrier and blacksmith.

Even if you are not convinced as to this argument, your spirits will be lifted when you reach Thieveley Pike. You soon leave the Rossendale Way, not long after Heald Top Farm, and strike up the hillside to join the Burnley Way (don't worry, it's less than half a mile with not a housing estate in sight). This leads to the top of the Pike and the view beyond. To the west is Pendle Hill with the hills of the Forest of Bowland looming behind it. To the north lie the Howgills and the Yorkshire Three Peaks, awaiting a much later return leg of the journey. The summits of the remaining three counties are over the horizon, but there is a sense that you have reached, if not the beginning of the end, at least the end of the beginning.

This is now the direction of travel and the Burnley Way drops steeply through Buckley Wood into another rift that allows various transport systems to shift people and goods across the Lancashire/Yorkshire border. In the present case, the A646, a train line from Preston to Leeds, and eventually the Rochdale Canal to Sowerby Bridge. Once the valley has been reached, you weave your way around the railway towards Burnley. At the foot of Thieveley Pike there is a curious system of bridge and tunnel that suggests a more intricate use might once have been practised.

Eventually, you arrive at the main road which, once crossed, leads you to another but more straightforward housing estate and the back door of the extensive Towneley Park and its Hall. For centuries the Towneleys were an important Catholic family who defied the reformation of the church in England. Eventually, the family's fortunes declined and the property was sold to Burnley Corporation, ghost and all, with the Hall opened as a museum and the grounds made free for public use. Follow the lengthy drive past the golf course to the front gates, where you step off the manicured verges into the back streets of Burnley.

So, trains and boats and plains it is, with more to come. I am not sure what exotic journey Billy J Kramer and the Dakotas had in mind as they recorded the lyrics of their hit record, but I am certain it was not a rather convoluted walk across the hinterland of industrial Lancashire.

— 3 —

Every which way
Burnley to Slaidburn

Burnley is the only town of any real size on this journey from Three Shire Head to Carlisle. It made its money out of textiles and at the height of its prosperity boasted a population of over 100,000. It was also an original member of the Football League and more than held its own when playing the so-called big clubs from the cities. The town's economic importance was sufficient to alter the intended course of the Leeds and Liverpool Canal which, as a result, went much further north than was originally planned. It may be that the early subscribers had a variety of motives for its construction but I imagine that forming a significant part of the Burnley Way was not one of them.

As it is, the towpath is quickly accessible from the gates of Towneley Hall and by the time we leave the banks of the waterway, Burnley has been virtually bypassed. The main feature of this section is a huge embankment on which the canal is perched sixty feet above the town in its efforts to maintain a level between Gannow Tunnel and Brierfield. Where the streets do rise to meet it, there is a conclave of decaying warehouses and empty wharves that combine to create a strangely peaceful canyon. The scene must have been very different in its heyday. Canals are now used, for the most part, for recreation and have become a regular calendar feature to depict rural England, a boat chugging between established trees, accompanied by the obligatory posse of ducklings. It is therefore hard to realise the extent of the turmoil in the eighteenth and nineteenth centuries when the construction of these conduits for long distance haulage disturbed the countryside and those who lived in it.

The Leeds/Liverpool was no exception. At 127 miles long, it was the first to attempt to cross the Pennines and forty years later was the last to finish the journey. The reasons for the delay were various. After the usual preliminaries, but before a Petition was presented to gain the necessary enabling Act, the problems started. Because of its complexity and length, the inevitable counter-petitions and objections were more numerous than usual. Adjacent land and mill-owners, fearing for their water supply, and rival rail and canal companies similarly jealous of their profits had to be appeased one way or another. Even the local populace, which should have benefited from better transport links, was sceptical, afraid that the cream of local produce would be whisked away from them to feed the ever-expanding cities. In addition, the scale of the grand design was such that many subscribers were needed from the very beginning, each bringing his or her own agenda to the table. Delays occurred and recurred as the exact route was debated, often requiring as a consequence the need to resurvey and seek fresh permission.

Nevertheless, the businessmen who dreamt up the project called a meeting at the Sun Inn, Bradford, to which particularly landowners, clerics and other gentry were invited. Eventually, sufficient subscribers and an engineer to survey the land were found and the Petition was put before Parliament. As already indicated, it was at this moment that the real shenanigans began. Bribery, ranging from offers of profit-sharing to straightforward backhanders, was necessary before work could commence. Yet even when outsiders were pacified, there was disharmony within the ranks. Some of the shareholders were interested in shifting goods around only their side of the Pennines and saw no necessity to indulge in extra expense through the construction of even more locks to carry the waterway over the backbone of England. In particular, one group felt that the effort should concentrate on trade between the cities of Liverpool and Manchester and the rich coalfields of Wigan. It had no objection to the canal's continuation into Yorkshire but felt that the compensation offered by shifting bales of shoddy and snub did not merit the cost of a lengthy detour via Burnley. The toys came out of the pram and subscribers withdrew their support. In the end, compromises were found and at last work could begin.

The entrepreneurs might well retire to their brandies and soda, content that all was resolved, but further problems remained on the ground. In addition to the usual engineering conundrums, gangs of men were required to shift soil and hack rock for every inch of the way. These 'navigators' were mostly Irish and Scottish immigrants, with a supplement of inveterate vagrants. They generally caused havoc. Not content with fighting amongst themselves (there was more than one public house that had separate entrances for Protestants and Catholics), they more often than not concentrated their efforts in an attack on the local populace. Fired by often justifiable grievances, they broke into public houses and stole beer by the barrelful. Fired by that, they roamed the town demanding food and money with menaces. The local constabulary was powerless and chaos reigned until the navvies moved on to the next section or the cavalry was sent for and the Riot Act read.

Today, the traveller can slip through the town unnoticed and once Barracks Station has been passed you are soon once more in the country. And in the countryside you will remain until you cross the M6 and enter Carnforth. As always, it is the actual getting away from civilisation that proves the problem. In this case you leave the canal at the first road bridge after crossing the M65 and head for the river Calder through the inevitable housing estate. Follow the path on its south bank until you can pick up a right of way that runs across the fields to the stables and nurseries. Skirt the wood to join a lane that descends past Hollins Farm to rejoin the river. After crossing the bridge you join the Pendle Way. At this point you also cross the Brontë Way, though I think it unlikely that Emily and sibs strolled out here from Haworth as a way of spending a summer's afternoon.

Set off up the hill to the village of Higham whose presence is first announced by the spire of St John the Evangelist. Where there is a church, the pub is not usually far off, in this case with the curious name of the Four Alls Inn. Closer inspection of the sign reveals all. It is divided into quarters depicting the human race: the king who rules all, the priest who prays for all, the soldier who fights for all, and the common man who pays for all. It was built in 1792 and for the twenty years before the Second World War housed the Higham Balloon Juice Company which, on the surface, seemed to be a legitimate enterprise with directors, AGMs and all the usual trappings. In fact, it was a spoof and had no more more substance than the ascent of Rum Doodle. Higham's other connection with myth and fairy tales was Anne Whittle (aka Chattox), one of the Pendle witches who, it was claimed, enlisted the help of the devil to turn the beer sour.

Behind the village runs the Roman road which connected Ribchester to Colne, but once the legions, having put in place their exit strategy, had tramped their last journey, the locals returned to the traditional practice of farming. Together with a bit of cottage industry, which in this part of the world was weaving, life evolved at a very sedate pace. But the changes that took place in the village between the middle of the eighteenth century and the present day affected most of the Pennine villages surrounding our walk and the transformations at Higham can be seen as typical of the greater picture.

The first significant change was caused by the invention of mechanical alternatives to hand spinning

Burnley to Slaidburn

and weaving. This increased productivity, but reduced the need for individual labour, and the consequent surplus of people seeking employment meant that owners of small mills could reduce wages. As this, in some instances, was by more than half, much poverty and distress ensued. Although offset to a certain extent by the expansion of the industry through exports to the burgeoning Empire, it caused a major social upheaval. People were forced to congregate and form communities where work was to be found. As a result, brickworks sprang up in Higham, as elsewhere, to provide new terraced accommodation for the incomers. When steam replaced water power, the mills flourished, not by the stream but where coal could be found. Further upheavals took place and the process started again.

Higham was lucky that it could stay put. Owing to the proximity of the mine sunk at Habergham, the two mills in Higham in their heyday contained 800 looms and employed 200 workers. When, forty years later, this fuel resource proved insuffucient, a drift mine was excavated at Fir Trees. The local economy boomed. Sixty years ago, the population had risen to 2,000. There were three clubs (Lib, Lab and Tory), a pub, village shop, Co-op, post office, cobbler, grocers/café, three butchers, a sweetshop, joiner and undertaker. The last time I passed through the village only the pub and village store/post office were left. The colliery closed in 1930 and the drift mine in 1966, both quickly to remerge into the landscape. The mills, in turn, were demolished and modern-day housing was put in their place. *O Tempora, O Mores*, as the good folk of Higham were wont to say.

Nowadays, there is not much to keep you as you cross the main street and leave Higham along a lane that runs to the left of St John's church. The land rises gently until it reaches the road to Newchurch. But the Pendle Way, sensing a shortcut, vaults a stile and crosses a pasture of gorse above Higher Town. Since leaving the Calder you have been climbing steadily, but such is the gradient that you probably failed to notice that you had approached the 1,000-foot contour for the first time since Thieveley Pike. Therefore it comes as a surprise to find that you are standing on the top of an incipient Pendle Hill. The real McCoy is not to be mistaken. It rises impressively before you out of its secret valley. Now, as you descend sharply into Sabden Fold, you should keep a weather eye open for low flyers, not RAF fighters but broomsticks, for this is Pendle Witch country.

Although the tale of the Pendle witches is well known, it is nonetheless an interesting passage in history, if only because it reflects considerable light on human behaviour. Substitute 'witchcraft' for any commonly felt fear, e.g. 'terrorism', and it is easy to see that the story belongs to all races and in all times. In the Pendle case, there was a group in the community, mostly women, who did not conform to accepted behaviour and as such were held in much suspicion. There is no doubt that in this case the women in question played on these fears for their own purposes, both individually and in immediate family groups.

Matters eventually came to head on 18th March 1612. Alizon Device cursed a pedlar, John Law, because he refused to sell her some pins. Whereon Law was struck with a seizure and collapsed. He quickly recovered but Device was clearly shaken by the apparent effect of her curse and apologised to Law, excusing herself on the grounds that she was a witch and 'other forces' had in that moment taken control. Law, no doubt somewhat shaken himself by the circumstances, accepted her apology and went on his way.

That might have been the end of the matter, but this seems to have been the moment others had been waiting for. Law's son, Abraham, was not so forgiving and reported Device's confession to the authorities. This set up a chain of arrests, interrogations and confessions that resulted in thirteen witches (eleven female, two male) being hanged by 30th August of the same year. Their supposed victims included seventeen human beings and a variety of livestock. The evidence was meticulously recorded by the Clerk to the Lancaster Assizes, who then rushed a book into print by the following November. Some things never change.

As we have already met Anne Whittle, the statements of 'Chattox' will do as well as any to demonstrate the nature of these 'confessions'. Chattox admitted that, some fourteen years previously, she had met a figure in the form of a man some three or four times. He eventually persuaded her to sell him her soul in return for his helping her to achieve whatever she wanted. She was to refer to him as 'Fancie'. The nub of the case against Chattox surrounded the death of a local landowner Robert Nutter. Nutter had tried unsuccessfully to seduce her daughter, Anne Redferne, who was already married. Repulsed, Nutter stormed out, threatening to get his own back. Chattox pre-empted such action by enlisting 'Fancie's' help and within three months Nutter was dead. The rest of the 'crimes' to which she confessed were for the most part limited to such heinous acts as charming the beer and inflicting evil spirits upon unfortunate cows.

The truth was rather more complicated. A number of people were involved in a land dispute with Nutter and if his death was from other than natural causes any of these could have been just as responsible as Chattox. In fact, the whole of the Pendle affair was internecine. There was a long-standing feud between the Whittles and the Southerns, another supposed coven of witches whose matriarch, known as Demdike, was the mother of Alizon Device. It had reached a particular head at this point as there was an ongoing struggle between Chattox and a female member of the rival family for the attentions of a man. Where there is a sect, sex is never far away.

So it is not surprising that, half-way through her confession, Chattox changed tack. Although still admitting her part, she shifted the blame to Demdike, with whom she had at one time been in cahoots, saying she had instructed her to kill Robert Nutter. For good measure she threw in another suspect, Margaret Pearson. Demdike had by this time conveniently died in gaol. Wherever the truth really lay, it had by then been camouflaged by superstition, rumour and spite.

To the modern mind, this sort of persecution seems bizarre and the punishment, inflicted on the strength of such flimsy evidence, barbaric but that is to look at it from a particular historical perspective. The outcome arose from a human condition that bestrides the ages, namely a desire to blame others for your own inadequacies and mistakes. As a result, as any football manager will tell you, scapegoats are sought upon whom you can vent your frustration. Why did the crops fail? Not because of your poor farming but because of the witches. Why should innocent people in Iraq die? Not because the oil supply is under threat but because persecuting their leader is the only way to free the world from terror. Where appropriate, toss in a dollop of greed and *schadenfreude* and stir until it bubbles.

In the scapegoat stakes, witches have traditionally found the going pretty heavy. There is no good without bad and the Christian church raised to an art form the naming and shaming of suitable scapegoats to explain the otherwise inexplicable disasters caused by its benign, all-loving god. Stalin was not the first to discover that having the moral police in your pocket was no bad thing. Furthermore, it would kill two birds with one stone if the church could show that independent-minded women were most often responsible. In early sixteenth-century England, matters were exacerbated by the morbid interest that James I showed in witchcraft. It never does your chances of enhancement any harm to find evidence to support the boss's beliefs and it comes in everyone's interest, except the victims, to out the witches whether astride their broomsticks or lurking under the bed.

When the pot has reached its critical heat, sprinkle a liberal handful of revenge, envy and jealousy with a drizzle of exploitation of opportunity and bring swiftly to the boil. For a dramatic exposition of the causes and effects of witchcraft there is no need to look further than a production of Arthur Miller's play *The Crucible*. Set in Salem, Massachusetts, at a similar moment in history, Miller constructs, as a parallel to illustrate the McCarthy witchhunts of the 1950s, an interweaving of character and circumstance that allowed spite and envy to prosper in the name of Puritanical Christian zeal. But this explanation still avoids the question as to why, when the evidence against them is based on nothing more substantial than circumstance and superstition, the Pendle witches confessed so readily.

Perhaps again the answer is found not so much through the particulars of this case but in an examination of human behaviour in general. Confessing to a crime that the accused did not commit is not unusual at any point in history. The simple explanation that the Pendle witches were tortured is simply not available, for unlike the Inquisition and Orwell's Room 101, torture was not generally used in England at that time to incriminate witches. Ministers may well have been more interested in saving their unfortunate souls than inflicting pain. In fact, such was the speed of events that there scarcely time to dust off the thumb screws, let alone use them. Perhaps the most likely explanation is that it was a perverse sort of pride and the women were up for their fifteen minutes of fame. Perhaps in their simplicity they had persuaded themselves and each other that they truly were accomplices of the Devil.

Your route has now taken you through Newchurch, past a shop, Witches Galore, with broomsticks (Full MOT Guaranteed) and other such Disneyfied paraphernalia for sale. We have nowadays trivialised the likes of Halloween and the Gunpowder plot and turned them into children's games. It makes you wonder whether our descendants will find similar substitutes to celebrate the horrors of 9/11 and global warming. The hill is ascended via Ogden Reservoir and Ogden Clough and when the angle eases and the summit plateau is reached, you join the Witches' Way that will lead to Slaidburn and the end of this section.

After a short distance of crossing rough moorland, the point that is Pendle End is reached, sporting an impressive cairn. And so it should, for this is a commanding position above the impressively steep drop that plunges onto the village of Barley with a fine panorama that takes in the hills of the Forest of Bowland, Lakeland's Central Fells and High Street before sweeping across Shap onto Ingleborough and the Yorkshire Three Peaks.

One of the less obtrusive bumps on the horizon is Gragareth, officially the highest point in the county through which you are now walking. It may stand 200 feet above the point you occupy but it is in no other way superior to Pendle Hill. When the County Top of Lancashire was the Old Man of Coniston, Pendle must have been happy to bend the knee, but must feel somewhat aggrieved that an Ossian Wart of Yorkie origin now takes precedence. For Pendle is a proper hill. Topographically at 1,827 feet, it commands the space between the hills of North Wales and those of the Lake District. Its summit plateau is four miles long but, unlike Ward's Stone which is a dozen feet higher, it is not a sprawling moor but a slender whaleback that falls steeply on all sides into the surrounding valleys.

It is time now to bid adieu to the Pendle Way

and continue on the Witches' Way that will guide you to Slaidburn. It is probably fair to point out that the Witches' Way, in terms of signposts and traffic, does not have the sort of backing and support of its predecessor. On the evidence of a couple of photocopied sides of A4, with a level of route detail that, at times, makes mine seem prolix, the Way is the product of local enthusiasts who probably decided that fifty kilometres was a decent day's walking. As a result, more care than usual is required to follow the best route. But such local enthusiasts are to be applauded if they keeps paths open and report disrepair to the relevant Highway Authority. If they didn't, it's unlikely the farmers would, and even less likely that the persons legally responsible for their upkeep would leave their centrally-heated offices to find out for themselves. Access to Open Countryside is all very well, but you've got to be able to reach it and when you can no longer perform mountain goat manoeuvres, it is nice if the stiles are kept in repair.

From the summit a concessionary path takes you off the hill to the road below. Paths then lead to the village of Downham, the location for Hayley Mills's film *Whistle Down The Wind*. Some more wriggling takes you by the church with its fifteenth-century tower and the Assheton Arms, named after and no doubt once owned by the local gentry, to reach the fields beyond. The route of the right of way has now been changed to avoid walking through someone's garden and instead passes the pub door. Clearly, vested interest had a part to play in this decision.

When you reach Newfield Farm, you leave the road that runs between Downham and Gisburn and pass under the railway that follows a similar line. This leads to Smithies Brook and another elegantly arched bridge. Though not on the same scale as that which carried the M62 over our heads, it, in its day, must have performed an equally valuable service. For the packhorse bridge must have saved as much time and trouble as its descendant, since a forced detour would have been both tedious and, if in the wrong place at the wrong time, dangerous. Smithies Brook Bridge is now within a peaceful hollow, but the name still suggests the ringing iron and flying sparks of another era. Rights of way lead over and through what were on my last visit ever more collapsible stiles to the busy A59, then through the monastic ruins to the rather superior Spread Eagle of Sawley.

Leave Sawley by the pleasant riverside paths of the Ribble until you gain the road at Bank House. The next bit can get a bit tricky. Finding Hill House is easy enough but very careful navigation and an indifference to mischievous stiles adorned with barbed wire is required if you are to reach the lane that circumnavigates Grindleton Forest. Local inclination tries to herd you in a rather different direction, but if you do go wrong and you have to resort to road walking, there is not that much of the black stuff and, as compensation, you pass a pleasant little pool with, according to season, a variety of wildfowl.

You have become so used to meadow-meandering since leaving Pendle Hill that the next bit comes as something of a surprise. Although the B6478 is never that far away, you quickly realise that you are entering a wilder country sprouting odd-shaped rocks and hidden pools, not to mention the curiously named Walloper Well, but it's only when you reach Far Brown Hill that you realise that you have once more overtopped 1,000 feet and are at the top of yet another steep descent, this time into what will become the Trough of Bowland. The helter-skelter starts again and the valley bottom and its river are reached by way of Padiham Barn, Easington Village and some pretty impressive stiles. Follow the river past Dunnow Hall and into Slaidburn and the open fires of the Hark to Bounty.

— 4 —

Birds, bogs and brass
Slaidburn to Wray

It was late on an autumn afternoon when I first stood on the flank of Easington Fell to gaze in the direction of Slaidburn. The sky was overcast and in the valley pricks of light were starting to appear. I looked at the ground that lay before me, then again at the map. The way forward did not appear obvious to the eye (no convenient signpost here) and, at least according to the Ordnance Surveyors, the drop was steep. Moreover, there were stiles to find and a river to cross before I could approach the road to my next meal and bed. These observations merely compounded the gathering gloom and sense of foreboding. The bard may have considered that discretion is the better part of valour but I suspect in Falstaff's case and know in mine that any pusillanimity was due more to decrepitude of body and spirit than measured judgement. I looked on the possibility of the tripwired tussock as Sir John had looked on the Gunpowder Percy.

Beside me there was a road covered in tarmac that I knew ran smoothly towards the hotel bar. Although, being two sides of a triangle, the distance was further, the time would probably be shorter and to wile away that time I could amuse myself with memories of how less discreet decisions had once almost caused benightment on Ben Hope and had prompted me in a white-out to slither down a six-foot drop that turned out nearer to sixty. It was only when I reached the hotel that I began to realise the downside of my triumph. If I were to prospect fully the right and proper way of my route, I must return to the top of the hill. If I took the car, I would have to walk back up again. If I left the car at the hotel, there would be a tedious slog before the day's real exploration began. Fortunately, the thing about the North is that strangers talk to each other and it wasn't long before I had arranged a lift for the morning.

My good samaritan had a car-that-whizzed, but before he smalled into the middle distance he got out of his vehicle to demonstrate the view, accompanying the scene with a suitably enthusiastic commentary. I had never heard the returning native wax as lyrical since I had been in the company of a man enhancing the bar profits of Caledonian MacBrayne on his way home to the island of Barra from the Scottish mainland. Today's annunciation might have been more succinctly delivered but the sentiment was the same. There he was born and there he would die. It was there he belonged.

For Slaidburn and its people have deep historical roots. 'Slateburn' appears in the Domesday Book. The church was linked to Pontefract Priory in the thirteenth century and a grammar school for suitably bright children was built in 1717 by John Bremnand. But there was much to-do before the Conquest. It had been ruled by Tostig, son of the Earl of Wessex, who was universally disliked and turfed back to where he belonged. It was also laid waste in 1061 by bands of marauding Scots and after the accession of William I, like most of Yorkshire, had its fair share of the Harrying of the North. To precede injury with insult, London had imposed a certain Costig upon them. Not only did he sound like the former dictator but was actually a student of his methods. Unsurprisingly, he didn't last long.

The Normans gave up what had turned out to be an unequal struggle and for a number of years the area turned into bandit country. Slowly prosperity was restored under the more benign rule of the remaining Anglo-Saxon thanes. The Forest of Bowland was declared a royal hunting ground and Slaidburn, with its Swaincote mote court, became the centre of a thriving community. The old courtroom can still be seen in the room above the bar of the Hark to Bounty in more or less its original state. Even today the area retains its independent turn of mind. The word 'clough', meaning a ravine, is generally pronounced to rhyme with 'cuff'. In this part of the world it rhymes with 'shoe'. Despite in-depth research by the University of Leeds and the Lancashire Dialect Society, no evidence can be adduced that it is so pronounced anywhere else in the North. Bowland, incidentally, is pronounced as the land of clogs and windmills.*

So 1974 must have come as a bit of a shock. As followers of this trail or, at least, the text will probably have realised, this was the year of the Great Boundary Change and one morning Yorkshiremen, who had defied all that various outside agencies could throw at them, woke up to discover that they had been turned into Lancastrians. The transformation must have been of Kafkaesque proportions as they slowly realised that now they would be expected to argue the case that Brian Statham was a better bowler than

*The author appreciates that the previous passage might well cause difficulties for any future translators, so would, albeit hesitantly, refer them to *English Etymology and Other Atrocities Inflicted upon the Human Race during the Expansion of the British Empire*, P V Privisci, Millrace 1984.

Fred Truman and accept that the proper response to the Loyal Toast was not 'The Queen' but 'The Duke of Lancaster'. Old wounds were reopened and this new attempt by southern politicians to disrupt the historical pattern in order to save their parliamentary seats must, again not surprisingly, have been greeted with some scepticism.

The situation reminds me of a story, doubtless apocryphal, told by my father. It concerned a friend of his from the Home Counties who decided to attend a Roses match at Old Trafford and sat between a Yorkshire and a Lancashire supporter. Yorkshire were batting and when Len Hutton struck an immaculate cover drive for four, my father's friend leapt to his feet and started applauding. A few balls later the batsman attempted a similar shot, but on this occasion it was anticipated by Eddie Paynter who swooped like a panther and whistled the ball back to the keeper before the batsman had completed the final flourish of his stroke. My father's friend repeated his performance, on this occasion adding, 'Oh, well fielded, sir!' After he had returned to his seat, the Lancastrian turned and asked him whether he came from Lancashire. When father's friend replied in the negative, the Yorkshireman enquired a touch more aggressively whether, in that case, he came from

Yorkshire. 'No,' came the reply, 'I'm just here to watch a jolly good game of cricket.' There was a very short pause, the sort of pause that is necessary to get a decent inhalation of breath before the unanimous outburst, 'Then, bloodywell shut up and sit still! It's nowt to do with thee.'

On that note, and particularly if you have been rather liberal with your views the night before, it is probably best for any visitor to have an early breakfast and quietly slip past the war memorial towards the bridge that crosses Croasdale Brook. This is the start of the next stage. But don't forget to take your free packed lunch for there is no chance of further sustenance until you reach Wray.

If you have picked the right day, another note— or rather series of notes—might strike you and if it sounds familiar, it is because it features not only in the repertoire of every brass band but also in the opening scenes of *The Full Monty*. 'Slaidburn' is a tune composed by William Rimmer, the greatest brass band composer and conductor of his day, whose reputation was secured when, under his tutelage, the Foden Motor Works Brass Band won the Grand Challenge Cup at Crystal Palace in 1909. Rimmer's mortal remains are buried in Slaidburn churchyard.

He arrived in the village to convalesce, but could not resist the chance to offer his services to the Slaidburn Silver Band. They, in turn, persuaded him to compose a piece especially for them and nowadays bandsmen come from all over the country to sit in and play 'Slaidburn' in Slaidburn. Although brass and silver bands are not exclusive to the North, they are always associated with the working classes and the North had its particular share of those. As we have seen, the Industrial Revolution had converted village life into collectives of mills and pits. This concentration produced a pool of local musical talent and 'masters' who, in the hope of enhancing their personal and commercial prestige, were prepared financially to support it.

The film *Brassed Off*, which is similarly themed to *The Full Monty*, tells the story of such a brass band whose members are faced with pit closure and job loss. Their plight acts as a metaphor for a Britain that was the victim of a political philosophy based on 'the fumblings in the greasy till' of the grocer's shop. Thatcherism seemed to take no account of the moral and social values that such communities had produced and in its place invented a Britain where the main beneficiaries resembled little more than a bunch of pumped-up adolescents jostling for the best view at a porn show. The film, less convincingly, has a Hollywood ending where the star-crossed lovers live happily ever after and the band wins the Grand Championship at the Albert Hall. In reality, a great majority of the voters were caught up in the North Sea Bubble of privatisation, share flotation and exploitation of housing equity. Inevitably it burst, taking with it whatever it was that Keir Hardie, those who fought in the Second World War and the inclusive social contract of the Attlee government were collectively striving for. After I had written this sentence, I read of a night-club in London that was offering for sale a single cocktail for £35,000, a sum greater than the annual wage of three-quarters of the population. Apparently there was no shortage of takers.

The best answer for nostalgic frustration, other than a cold shower, is vigorous exercise and therefore it's about time this narrative got back on the road. The road in question is the Hornby Road, an ancient trackway that crosses the heights of the Forest of Bowland. You reach it from the Croasdale bridge by heading north along field paths to the farm at Shay House. These then swing west until they reach the tarmac on Wood House Lane. At a gate at the end of the lane you join the Roman road that is, similarly to ourselves, travelling from Manchester to Carlisle, in its case to form a suitable supply line for the troops manning Hadrian's Wall.

For the last couple of miles you have been following the North Bowland Traverse, a product from the same stable as the Witches' Way. The aim of David Johnson and Jim Ashton was to design 'a continuous route from industrial Greater Manchester ... into the heart of the Yorkshire Dales'. But immediately after passing through the gate you are faced with a choice. Either follow the more circuitous but pleasant route of the Traverse over Dunsop Fell and up the Whitendale valley or, alternatively, *Via Directa Romana* along the Hornby Road. The former route has the added distinction of passing near the spot which is the exact centre of Britain (this is ascertained, incidentally, by balancing a cardboard cut-out of the Isles on the point of a pin). Not especially rewarding, other than to give you an interesting gloss on the phrase 'in the middle of nowhere'. Whichever way, you will meet yourself somewhere in the vicinity of Salter Fell.

You are now well established within the Forest of Bowland, a pretty big chunk of land that spreads from the M6 in the west into what was Yorkshire in the east. Our route, like the Roman road before us, creeps over the far eastern shoulder before descending

Slaidburn to Wray

into the Lune valley, leaving vast tracts of land to be explored on some other day. But 'another day' is another reason why I decided to do this walk. Over the years I have visited much of the high land and coast line of northern England, yet I was surprised how much I had missed or seen only from a particular viewpoint. A little thought tempered this surprise when I considered how long Wainwright took in fathoming out just the Lakeland Fells. That puts the extent of the northern heights into some perspective. There are nearly as many separate hills over 2,000 feet in the Pennine chain as there are in the Lakes and there is a good deal of distance between most of them. If you do something like the route described in the two volumes of this book, you quickly realise that further exploration of the country you are passing through could fill up your diary for some time to come.

A return visit to Bowland certainly pays dividends, particularly if a sense of remoteness appeals to you. Only those who yearn for the chummy crowds on Kinder or the summit cairn of Scafell Pike on August Bank Holiday Monday will be disappointed with these moors. Even today, they are little visited beyond the obvious attractions of Ward's Stone and the Hornby Road. I suspect the truth is that the brooding hills to the east of the M6 between Junctions 32 and 34 are hardly noticed in the holiday scramble to Ambleside and, for serious walkers intent on adding more Corbetts and Munros to their collection, it is far too early in the journey north to halt their progress. Like the Southern Uplands, the Northern Pennines tend to be bypassed in the mad rush to 'better things'.

Historically, there was another reason why few people visited the area. Abbeystead, an estate of some 23,000 acres, including much ground that is of interest to the walker, was owned by the Duke of Westminster and His Grace was not at all keen on his grouse being disturbed by the proletariat. The response to his attitude was similar to that which provoked the mass trespass further south but with considerably less success. In the first place, the protesters were fairly thin on the ground, with no nearby cities to swell their number, and second and more importantly, the established aristocracy were more adept and experienced at keeping the mob at bay than some jumped-up parvenu who had made a few bob out of the rag trade.

This was the Forest of Bowland and 'Forest' meant not a plethora of trees but was etymologically derived from *foris*, meaning land that could not easily be cultivated and had been given over to hunting.

The Norman kings were rather partial to hunting, in their case deer, and by the thirteenth century thirty percent of England was Royal Forests protected by a police force of foresters. Their rule was reinforced by Forest Courts, such as that in Slaidburn, which had draconian powers to deter poachers or local villagers who had the nerve to infringe the royal rights of the Forest. Although the present owner no longer has the opportunity of dismembering various parts of the anatomy to deter any offence against his rights to vert (as in allowing your pig illegally to eat His Grace's acorns), there was a sense of continued tradition in these parts that had not been vastly disturbed by the Industrial Revolution. Until the Access Bill was passed, much of the grounds, with the exception of a few concessionary paths, was strictly out of bounds.

Although the other major landowner, North West Water, was more tolerant, grouse shooting and its attendant income were jealously guarded throughout the region and it was a long way to drive to be turned back at the first stile. Particularly as the Howgills and Eastern Fells were just up the road. And then there was the Bowland Bog. For the more sartorially inclined, the place has its limitations. Proper 'blanket bog' is a mixture of sphagnum moss and bog pools several yards across. It is ombrotrophic, that is to say it is fed by rain and the required rainfall to satiate its appetite is 160 days per year. It may appear uninviting to the eye (or even thigh if you are unlucky) but its ecological importance is of the first order. It acts as a carbon plughole and is to Europe what the Amazonian rain forest is to South America in that it converts the carbon dioxide into oxygen. Experienced walkers in this country may not be surprised to learn that Britain has ten percent of all such bogs in the world.

But the history of the human race is littered with examples of settling for short-term solutions that create long-term problems. The infrastructure is of a fragile nature and is breaking down to be replaced by dry crumbling peat. Various reasons have been given for this. Poorly managed heather-burning, overgrazing by sheep and draining or bulldozing the moors to bolster the grouse industry have all been cited and, no doubt, jubilantly seized upon by the pro-accessors to strengthen their case. But there is another reason. The greatest single eroder of the landscape is man and now the struggle for access has been resolved in favour of social equality, it is time to take stock of both sides of the bargain. With privilege comes responsibility and somebody, preferably all parties involved, has to take responsibility for the protection of the countryside.

A good place to start from might be the premise that the individual has no more right to walk where he or she wants than another individual has a right to stop them. Bowland is relatively undamaged by human footfall and could become a model for good practice. The chattering classes who wave their forks in the air as they discuss the morality of hunting down defenceless creatures whilst tucking into their venison paté conveniently forget that the grouse moors sustain the local economy to a standard where it is possible (more fork-waving) to find a decent meal and a safe spot to park the 4 x 4.

Some matters are straightforward—agreeing on points of access and giving adequate and proper notice when the land can legitimately be closed—but any long-term plan must include a proposition that from time to time areas have to be shut off from the public to allow the landscape to recover. Most hill walkers, like sheep, follow the same trod, first wearing a way through the vegetation, then, when that gets muddy, seeking comfort on the fringes where the moor is desperately trying to re-establish itself. Snow and remoteness of access have saved most of Scotland from the worst of these intrusions but for the rest of Britain there are no such escape routes and, as the number of hill walkers increases, it may be that we will have to accept the rotation of our leisure opportunities as once we accepted the rotation of our crops.

When it came to owning land, there was no doubt that it was the rich what got the gravy—but it was not only the poor that got the blame. Raptors are the natural enemy of the grouse and therefore the owner. In particular, the hen harrier, an expert smash-and-grab merchant of the grouse chick, was singled out for retribution. As the witches before them, the harriers did not have a good press and whereas statistically there is sufficient suitable territory to sustain 200–250 breeding pairs in England, in fact there are only ten to twenty. There seems an odd circularity about a sporting regime that kills harriers to protect baby grouse that grow into grouse sufficiently large for the sportsman to blow them out of the sky to make the money to pay for a sporting regime...

The Bible (aka the Game Book) in the Abbeystead Estate Office, which keeps track on the annual avicide rate with an accuracy that would appear to do credit to a coroner's office, notes that the record for a shooting party of the traditional eight guns was 2,929. It is unlikely that a hen harrier, even with the help of seven of its pals, could lay waste in such a spectacular fashion or in so short a time. Moreover, like the rest of us, the harrier has a varied diet and is instrumental in removing a variety of small mammals that, left to their own devices, would have deterred the transformation of grouse eggs into the unwitting participants of the celebratory fly-past that honours the glorious twelfth. But the pendulum swings and legislation has been passed to protect the hen harrier and hill walker alike. Of course, traps are still laid and plots hatched by the haves to keep the have-nots at bay, but at least the cards are more evenly distributed. Symbolically, another celebration was held on the Abbeyfield Estate to mark the passing of the Access Act. As to what the hen harrier did, there is no record.

After passing Salter Fell, proceed along the well-made track to Higher Salter. Navigation is simplicity itself and so, unlike the rest of Bowland's moor, you are sure to meet a variety of people employing a variety of locomotion. On my first winter excursion, I came across four stallions steaming, three bikers bobbling, two joggers jigging and a posh chap in a Cherokee. Very festive. After you surmount the final stile that separates the track from Higher Salter Farm and study the map, you will notice that the next two hamlets are called Middle Salter and Lower Salter and, having already ascended Salter Fell, your curiosity might be aroused. This is the main thoroughfare from Whalley Abbey to Lancaster and points north for the transportation of salt. Whalley and other similar Abbeys were the crucial staging posts in the salt's journey from the Cheshire wiches and explain why the Bishops of Chester claimed the narrow corridor that runs up to the Yorkshire border between Derbyshire and Lancashire. This in turn explains why Black Hill was for a long time Cheshire's highest summit. It is most probable that the salt that travelled along this way was sea salt from Morecambe Bay, but it would be nice to think that our way may have been the Cheshire salters' way. They would have used highways wherever possible, but if they wanted to take the shortest as well as the quickest route, there was little in the way of alternative. I have estimated that the journey to this point on foot is roughly ninety miles. To reach the same places by car, albeit more smoothly, would be in the region of 130.

There would be little doubt as to which way the packhorses would go from here—straight down the Hornby Road. You have a choice. Either to take the high road or avoid the tarmac by continuing on the North Bowland Traverse to Harterbeck Farm, thereafter following field paths until they join a minor road a mile south of Wray. Normally, I would avoid the road wherever possible, but there is a case for making this an exception. The high road commands extensive views to the east and has little traffic. Whereas the way across tufted grass and bog can be time-consuming in what is already a quite long day. Moreover, the cross-country route can be impeded by portable electric fences that are moved about the fields to facilitate stock control and, unless someone has replaced the bridge, Goodber Beck can be quite tricky to cross after rain. The choice again is yours. Above or below the salt, as you see fit.

— 5 —

A brief encounter
Wray to Kents Bank

Whichever way to Wray, the bulk of Ingleborough is fast disappearing over your left shoulder. First seen from Thieveley Pike, it has been a landmark for a good number of miles on your way north and it will be a good few more before you finally set foot on its summit during the return journey. Of more immediate interest is the steepening ravine that houses the river Roeburn. On most occasions this meandering stream scarcely deserves such an imposing title, but appearances can be deceiving, as the villagers of Wray found to their cost one late summer's afternoon in 1967.

The early summer had been wet. In particular, the month of May had been the worst for two and a half centuries. What in effect was lying on and in the Forest of Bowland was a great reservoir held in place by the blanket bog. On 8th August the rain poured down on the bloated peat. A conservative estimate was three inches in two hours and local peculiarities might have meant that in some spots more than half again might have fallen in an even shorter time.

Eventually whatever had acted as a dam, burst and the already agitated Roeburn became a torrential cascade. It gathered speed and reinforcements as it poured past the Salters, before being momentarily checked by Barkin Bridge and the rising land that stood in its immediate path. Swerving to its right, it picked up Goodber Beck and all the waters above it to plough a furrow through the woodlands that lined its banks. Each obstacle offered no more than a momentary pause to build the weight of the river's ferocity and supplement its armoury with an immense battering-ram of timber. Until, at last, all gave way before it and, as the Assyrian, it fell like a wolf on the fold that was Wray.

In all, a farm, thirteen houses and seven bridges were swept away or damaged beyond repair. The full story is told in *The Wray Flood of 1967* in which Emmeline Garnett gathers eye-witness accounts of that day. One of most dramatic of these is recounted by Bill Brown. Backsbottom Farm was the only group of buildings that lay directly in the path of the torrent before it reached Wray. Bill had decided, with the help of neighbour Len Richardson from nearby Stauvin Farm and Len's nephew Harry Martin, that this was the day for the annual dipping of his ewes and lambs. They had just stopped for a cup of tea when it started to rain very heavily and the waters began to rise rapidly. It wasn't long before the men realised that they had to loose the sheep to their own devices and drove the ewes towards higher ground, but as Bill went back to free the lambs and help them to safety, the pen walls started to collapse. He escaped in the nick of time and sought refuge in the house. His last sight, as he turned before entering, was the pen walls being swept aside and forty to fifty helpless lambs being bundled head over heels down the valley.

His wife, Alice, was already upstairs and he joined her at the bedroom window to watch his farm being systematically dismantled. They clung to each other, feeling that their end had come and, if that were so, determined to die together. The water beneath them, smashing the downstairs windows and trying to batter the walls into submission, was a deep peaty brown, for its tidal wave had torn off the surface of the moor that lay in its path, rolling it up before it as you would roll a carpet. At last, the tumult lessened and what remained of the once submerged farming implements began to poke through its surface. Eventually the waters subsided sufficiently for the Bentham Fire Brigade to find a way to the house and rescue the couple from a landing outside their bedroom door. The stairs had gone. Bill's sense of relief was then replaced by one of guilt. For he had seen no sign of Len or Martin after they had released the ewes and if his neighbours had been swept away, he felt he would be to blame for asking them to be in that particular spot at that particular time. Fortunately, Len and his nephew had managed to reach higher ground and make their way to Wray. Of Backsbottom, very little in the way of buildings, machinery or livestock was left.

Although Act of God is a convenient get-out clause for insurance companies, it cannot be regarded as an entirely satisfactory explanation. Particularly if the explanation might lie a little closer to home. Anyone who is acquainted with the west of Scotland or the rockier parts of North Wales will be well aware that if there is no vegetation to hold the rain, streaming torrents can appear from nowhere and what was skipped over the night before has to be waded waist-deep the next morning. Among its many dubious charms, the blanket bog is so constructed as to hold gallons of water and thus prevent flash floods of this kind. But nature's defences only work if they are left alone. Activity by humans such as overgrazing, the collection of water and altering the ground to facilitate the massacre of game birds, can unwittingly tip the balance. Given the manner in which we have so far treated our environment, it would be unwise to assume that what appears to be the Hand of God is anything more or less than the hamfist of man.

And finding yourself waist-deep on that fateful day was not confined to the inhabitants of Wray. Even greater damage, fortunately not of inhabited areas, was inflicted on the land surrounding the Forest. But there were exceptions. Not far from Wray, the beck at Claughton caused a similar flood and mud and debris blocked a section of the A683, the main road from Lancaster to Kirkby Lonsdale. Firemen from the Bentham Brigade were again called to the rescue and Garnett's book contains a photograph of a man submerged to his waist being pulled out of the mud. In the Fenwick Arms, which lay directly in the firing line, a stripe marking the height of high water is drawn above the mantelshelf of a not insubstantial fireplace. But times have passed and the Fenwick Arms is now renowned as the headquarters for the Campaign for Real Gravy and for food inspired by a makeover achieved through a visit from celeb chef Gordon Ramsay and his Kitchen Nightmares. It seems worth a visit. You don't find Goosnargh Cornfed Chicken and Chovizo Salad on many bar menus.

Suitably forewarned, you resume your travels along a system of streams and rivers until you finally escape onto the high ground of your final push west. Leave Wray by a choice of paths, crossing the track of a long-gone railway that used to run from Lancaster to Wennington. Eventually you join the river Hindburn which, in turn, flows into the Wenning. Pass Hornby Castle, a faux gothic mansion built around a Norman keep, and through Bridge Farm into Hornby. Cross the bridge and continue along the river bank to where the Wenning joins the Lune. Here turn north towards Loyn Bridge. All very straightforward except for a couple of points. The first is an inconvenient but mercifully short stretch of overgrown crumbly-banked woodland just before the bridge. The second is that your exit route lies under its arch and is very close to river level. If in doubt, look for an alternative that exists at a higher level. If in doubt, think Wray, think Fenwick Arms!

It was at this point that I had to make a planning decision as to which way to go. The required destination was Arnside, as it was from there I intended to cross Morecambe Bay. The obvious way would be to follow the Lune to Kirkby Lonsdale, then pick up the Limestone Link that reaches the coast via Hutton Roof and an old coffin route. I decided, however, to cut the corner via Carnforth and Silverdale. This decision was not born entirely out of idleness but a desire to look at the lump of land that lies to the west of the M6. As with the Forest of Bowland, this is also usually bypassed in the mad dash north but I had heard interesting reports which I had long hoped to investigate. But there was a drawback attached to the immediate part of that route. A glance at the map shows that such rights of way as exist are comparatively thin on the ground and tend to lie across rather than in the intended direction of travel.

The whole thing could be avoided by marching the half-dozen or so miles of road that separate Loyn Bridge from Carnforth but I took comfort that others, more approved than I, had not shirked a similar challenge. Wainwright, in his otherwise excellently thought-out and constructed Coast to Coast Walk, had been faced with a similar, if somewhat more lengthy problem when attempting to cross the hill walkers' desert that lies between Richmond and Ingleby Cross. His first tactic was to admit the truth: 'If you are fond of placid rural scenery and have an interest in farming, you might enjoy this section of the walk; but if your preference is for high ground and rough hills you will find it tedious,' and suggesting that 'the best way to cover these twenty miles ... is to get them over quickly by use of country lanes and roads.' And then, more succinctly: 'rights of way are suspect

Wray to Kents Bank

Keserve
ton
1

Kellet

er
Kellet

Loyn Bridge

Aughton

Hornby
River Wenning

River Lune

WRAY

River Roeburn

High Salter

G.R.Dale
Mar '08

or at best wasteful of time'. To fill this hiatus before the Blue Bell is reached, his reader is taken on a tour of a Memorial Obelisk that celebrates the incredible longevity of one Henry Jenkins (1500-1670), the site of the Battle of Standard (1138) and the highways and byways of the English Legal System as it relates to Rights of Way. It appeared to me that the author hoped that, with these inclusions, the barbed wire fences, collapsible stiles and overinquisitve bovines might conveniently slip the memory.

Armed with this precedent, I likewise decided to make the best of a bad job and recalled some details of a book I had picked up on my travels entitled *Rambles Twixt Pendle and Holme* by Joe Bates. He describes his walks in some detail at a time when walking along country lanes was a pleasure rather than a hazard and he clearly hoped to see examples of the wildlife he listed in his appendices. I, too, hoped that the said wildlife in my caesura had not cottoned onto the fact that their habitat was in danger of being disturbed on a regular basis, and that this section, although not of the first water in Alpinism, would be similarly rewarding. Bates listed sightings of a sea eagle on Pendle Hill in 1884, as well as great northern divers and snowbunting. Apart from the aforementioned fauna, flora was also abundant, with the author noting the existence of 500 species of flowering plants and shrubs, including the rare pheasant's eye and dusky cranesbill, never forgetting, of course, the much-loved melancholy thistle. He also observed that fig trees continued to grow wild.

I had hoped that my reported observations, like AW's bits of trivia, would do in place of a detailed celebration of this stage of the journey. My optimism, however, was misplaced. It did not help that, initially, I was forced to follow the Lune in entirely the wrong direction in order to reach the village of Aughton and a suitably orientated footpath. The way now weaves along a series of field paths and judicially selected stretches of road, sidestepping between, on one hand, a partially built pipeline, the purpose of which seemed to be to provide a suitable shelter for the workforce to play cards, and, on the other, a variety of irritating livestock. To make matters worse, I had decided to explore the crossing during the monsoon season and the rain, if not merciless, was certainly not of the 'droppeth as gentle' variety. In such weather sensible flora and fauna tend to shut up shop, so there is little to report other than the odd bedraggled dog rose. Suffice to say, the highlight of the odyssey was a stile near Sidegarth that looked as if it could have been constructed by Isambard Kingdom Brunel.

As I bypassed whatever might be of interest in Nether Kellett, with a sharp right turn down the lugubrious Back Lane, I must admit I was getting a little depressed with dodging frisky bullocks and juggernauts driven at anything other than a funereal pace. I went round a bend to the top of a slight rise. The rain had stopped and the light was beginning to clear. It was then I had what Wordsworth might have described as a daffodil moment. A newly polished Morecambe Bay lay before me and beyond it the Lakeland fells. Not even the army of Xenophon greeted the sight of the sea with such relish, for I had crossed Lancashire, and the Cumbrian mountains seemed tantalising close.

In reality, there was still a fair way to go but it was all downhill. A footbridge takes you over the M6 and paths take you past Thwaite House Farm and onto the Lancaster Canal. Follow the towpath past the Canal Turn until you reach Carnforth. No more boats or plains and only the occasional train for some time to come. Even after half a century, the mention of Carnforth causes alarm bells ominously to ring. Before the construction of the M6, the journey from the South to the Lakes on a Bank Holiday weekend made Pilgrim's Progress appear like a Sunday stroll. Amongst the various sloughs of despond were the traffic lights at Carnforth. Levens Bridge may have held the palm in many people's eyes, but in mine the inevitable delay at Carnforth was a worthy contender. So it was, as I pressed the button to demand right of way for the pedestrian, I hoped, on this occasion, it would be a somewhat briefer encounter.

Nowadays people actually go out of their way to get to the town in the hopes of experiencing another kind of *Brief Encounter*. Carnforth Station was the setting for the David Lean film of that name. The script, adapted from a one-act play by Noel Coward entitled *Still Life,* is a love story between a man and a woman who are already married. They first meet in the station refreshment room of 'Milford Junction'. Eventually they accept what they see as the inevitable and part, presumably, for ever.

The film was shot during a bitter February in 1944 when V1s and 2s were still falling on southern Britain, which was why Carnforth was chosen rather than a location within easier reach of the fleshpots of London. Filming requires a blaze of light that for obvious reasons could not happen at a critical railway junction within range of Hitler's rockets. Amongst the possibilities approved by the War Department, the director preferred Carnforth, as the sloped approach to the subway down which Laura had to run was easier to negotiate than the flight of steps normally found elsewhere. He probably thought that the line that curves gently out of view would be evocative of the emotional partings that many of his audience had recently experienced.

Not that these reasons, initially, appealed to the leading lady Celia Johnson. She was primarily a stage actress and had to be persuaded to take part in any film, let alone one where she had, as she wrote to her husband, 'to go up North for four weeks location on some horrible railway station'. Her attitude soon changed and, as she later reported, she was enjoying herself chatting to the locals, playing poker with the crew and warming herself between takes before the Station Master's office fire. She even went so far as to describe her benefactor as 'an old fashioned gentleman'.

Today the film has a certain cachet. Cinema buffs have spotted that in the opening shots the express apparently travelling north was in fact a reversal of the negative of a southbound train and that Carnforth Station stars for 523 seconds out of the 4920 selected to entertain the public. But these efforts were not appreciated at the time. Those treated to a preview, instead of being suitably moved, laughed at the love scenes. Presumably the deprivations 'recently experienced', being more violent than nostalgic, had dampened the enthusiasm for Coward and Rachmaninov amongst the inhabitants of Rochester.

Your exit towards Arnside begins in a similarly gloomy fashion, wending its way past a scrapyard towards the village of Warton, which once housed the ancestors of George Washington. You aim for paths that pass through Scout Wood and into the grounds of Leighton Hall. A dead end road leads past a rather good pub, the New Inn at Yealand Conyers, to reach Leighton Moss Nature Reserve. This is the only place in the North where bittern, marsh harriers and bearded tits still breed. A causeway with a public hide crosses the estuary which takes you to Silverdale Station. Once there, you cross the golf course and a network of paths allows a variety of approaches to Arnside. The most direct way is through Eaves Wood, a caravan site and past Arnside Tower, before skirting Arnside Knott and dropping into the town. It is a decent excursion for the daytrippers who want to walk one way, then catch a train back to their starting point, but there is much more to Silverdale than this.

It has been designated an Area of Outstanding Natural Beauty and, like the Forest of Bowland, is worthy of a more lengthy visit. My 'Direct Route' misses the Giant's Seat, a Victorian Pepperpot, and the Fairy Steps, a narrow cleft in the rock which, if climbed without touching the sides, will grant you a wish. Not too flattering an encounter for adults with delusions about waist size. Nor will you see the other four peel towers or Lindeth Tower, where Elizabeth Gaskell wrote some of her novels. A mad dash will most probably miss the hill fort of the Brigantes (300 BC), roe deer, red squirrels, nesting peregrine falcons and the rare high brown fritillary, and certainly the renowned view from the top of Arnside Knott. If all that begins to pall, there are walks along the foreshore and cliff tops. It says a good deal about the planning regulations of this country that somebody allowed an area set aside because of its natural beauty to be desecrated by three caravan sites and a golf course.

But the important thing is to end at Arnside, to enable a safe crossing of Morecambe Bay. It must be emphasised that the crossing is potentially a very dangerous affair and should be attempted only with an experienced guide. There are two types of danger—drowning and disappearing without trace in quicksands. Neither offers a particular advantage. The crossing, however, has been a trade route from time immemorial as it was an important short cut to link the system of abbeys that existed in the area.

The abbots, no doubt, knew the score. The bay can only be crossed during a couple of hours each side of low tide and after the official guide has inspected the course and decided on the safest route for that particular day. For such is the movement of the sands that what was sound enough yesterday can be a death trap tomorrow.

The official guide was appointed by the Duke of Lancaster and each day he rode out into the bay on his horse, prodding the ground with his staff and marking the route with bunches of twigs. Currently the office is held by Cedric Robinson who, on the appointed days, leads large groups, usually sponsored in the aid of some charity, and the simplest, if not quietest, way to effect the crossing is to join one of these. Cedric, staff aloft, sets off like some modern-day Moses and we follow to the promised land of lakes and fells. The safe extremities of each critical point are marked by a bush (not burning) somewhat incongruously planted some hours before. A halt is called and the party is ordered to spread into a long thin line to prevent the crossing point being churned into all-consuming quicksand. This is the cue for the children in the party to jump up and down on the same spot to test the theory. The Kent Channel, which can be ankle- or thigh-deep depending on previous weather, has to be crossed before reaching the safer ground of the mudflats. The party, with many thanks, gains the station at Kents Bank, where, for the most part, it embarks on the next train travelling south.

It is when you are halfway across that you realise the hidden danger. Even on the finest of days, this is not like walking along a gently inclined beach where the incoming tide washes the toes with modest eddies. Sea-level is actually above you, with the waters held back by a series of sand bars. Once the tide rises above the rim of that basin, it floods the bay in a rush. If you stand on the mainland cliffs and watch the incoming tide, you realise the speed of its approach which, it is said, will outstrip a galloping horse. In competent hands there is little problem, but if caught in the wrong place at the wrong time there is no high ground of safety for the Lens and Martins stranded in Morecambe Bay.

— 6 —

A variety of secret waters
Kents Bank to Coniston

After the hordes have departed on the Manchester-bound train, you may find a sudden quiet descend. A silence that will be rarely disturbed by human agitation until you reach the popular resort of Coniston. Kents Bank, like much of the Sud-Lakeland that you are going to cross, is not, even in summer, a hive of tourist activity. But you have not been cast adrift entirely, for you have landed on your feet on the Cumbrian Coastal Way. An initial look at the map shows that any direct route is right-of-way-proof and that you may be consigned to tarmac-tramping once again. But the Coastal Way, if somewhat circuitously, will keep this to a minimum and eventually launch you on your journey north. It is also worthwhile in itself and allows you to examine Morecambe Bay at leisure, without fear of being swept off your feet.

A road leads uphill out of the village before the Way twists back on itself to return to the coast via Wyke and a small tunnel under the railway line. A permissive path follows the coast to join a footpath which leads to a minor road. This, in turn, circumnavigates Cark Airfield until you can join a public footpath linking West Plain Farm and Sand Gate. Thereafter, an enclosed country lane to Cark.

The whole affair, though short, is not without merit. However, most of the interest lies off stage. To the north of Humphrey Head is Wraysholme, home to the Harrington family, and it is reported that John, son of Sir Edgar H, killed, hereabouts, the last wolf in England. The official brochure of the Way instructs the walker not to disturb the wildlife along the shore of the Leven Estuary. Although you could be forgiven for assuming that this injunction refers to the cows and their offspring that patrol the causeway in a rather proprietorial manner, it in fact concerns the great variety of wading birds that breeds or winters on the saltmarshes. But these are not the only frequenters of the bay. Cocklers and shrimpers still ply their trade from the ancient Charter Borough of Flookburgh and it was a rite of passage among the young men to race the incoming tide across the bay. The more fleet of foot made it. The less quick, it may be assumed, ended up dead. The bartailed godwits were, no doubt, confused.

Cark, also, is an interesting place, if only through the mirror of history. The airfield was a fighter station and a training school for anti-aircraft gunnery crews.

Kents Bank to Lowick Bridge

As the threat of invasion receded, it became the base for what was to become the RAF Mountain Rescue Unit, the original purpose of which was to search for survivors of crashed planes rather than the foolish and benighted. But Cark's heyday was further back in time. Although it is now difficult to imagine, it was once a thriving commercial centre. A boatyard supplied the needs of the essential transport service that plied its trade up and down the Lancashire coast. But, like Arnside, its importance as a port was swiftly curtailed by the shifting sands and the arrival of a railway. There were also the inevitable mills, one for paper, the other for cotton. The latter was water-driven with the latest in technology (a fire engine invented and supplied by James Watt) which pumped the water back to the pound. Local archives show that there was a fair amount of espionage as Watt's competitors slunk around the premises trying to steal his design. Now the pleasant Engine Inn is the only obvious reminder of the past.

The next step from Cark to Cartmel is easily done along a path that lies to the west of the river Lea. This ends at a surprisingly spacious and verdant enclosure which leads with little problem to the village. Unless, of course, it happens to be a Bank Holiday, when you might get trampled to death. For the ground you are in the process of crossing is Cartmel racecourse. In that event, the village is anything but a quiet place as 20,000 people try to converge on this quiet corner of

Cumbria. As a top jockey put it, it is the only course, other than Cheltenham, where to make certain you don't miss it, you have to arrive three hours before the first. But race days are few and far between and for the most part it is a tranquil enough place. A variety of hotels, antiquarian bookshops and a twelfth-century priory set the mood.

Cartmel Priory was founded for the Augustines by William Marshal and was steadily augmented over the years. The wolf-slayers were clearly benefactors and Lord Harrington, having provided a chapel with four traceried windows, was buried in the church for his pains. The remarkable thing is that at the time of the dissolution of the monasteries, the church was not destroyed along with the rest of the buildings. The residents of Cartmel petitioned that, as Marshal had dedicated an altar within the priory to the village, thus rendering a further church superfluous, this was their only place of worship. The petition was received successfully and the church was spared. Mind you, four monks and ten villagers were hanged to discourage the practice from becoming a habit. During the seventeenth century it was used as a stable for the military, a prison and a grammar school. There was then no further degeneration in use and the dust gradually settled.

Perhaps it was that tranquillity that attracted a coterie of poets and writers at the beginning of the last century. The father figure was George Bottomley, a Georgian poet who had set up house at Well Knowe in 1892. Younger men, like the poet Edward Thomas and Lascelles Abercrombie, who later gained some renown as a critic and academic, sought Bottomley's advice and, no doubt, influence in the world of letters. Amongst these was Arthur Ransome, who had been commissioned to find young authors to produce a series of prose volumes and considered Wall Nook at Cartmel a suitable place to set up his headquarters.

The next stage of our journey to Coniston is via Lowick Bridge at the foot of Coniston Water. In the beginning, we follow a route much trodden by Ransome and his various acquaintances and, like them, set off once again across the racecourse in the direction of Bottomley's house. The route is directed through a steep wood and Well Knowe is soon reached. Field paths lead from there to Wall Nook. But on many occasions, sometimes with Lascelles, sometime alone, Ransome pushed on further north. And it is this route of his that we shall also follow, but probably for rather different reasons.

Although the likes of Thomas tended to treat him as he might a younger brother and Ransome appeared the least likely amongst the group to be a roaring literary success, first impressions were confounded. It seems that he, like many young men of his age, aspired first and foremost to become a poet and he had not realised that the country he was passing through was to become the bedrock, literally in the case of the knickerbocker breaker, of his later fame and fortune. His road to this end had also been a rocky one. His father died when he was still quite young and his mother, understandably enough, was anxious that he should follow a financially reliable profession. Even more understandably, she did not regard a career as a writer as falling into that category. A Bohemian life in London, followed by an unsuccessful marriage and trips to Russia during the Revolution, where he met and played chess with Lenin, provided obvious fodder for any later writings but in fact it was his more homely forays into the Lake District that did the trick. But these were things to come. He took and now we follow a short stretch of road, then the large wood of the Great Allotment, before passing a picturesque little tarn that might well, at a much later date, have worked its way into one of his stories.

And it was one consequence of his eventual decision to concentrate on children's literature that I, as a child, unleashed my hoarded birthday money and bought a book because it had maps for endpapers and the intriguing title of *Secret Water*. I hadn't read far before I discovered that what I held in my hands was a cut above the average Christmas fodder. It was clear that this was one of a series that was in full swing and I was anxious to discover the whereabouts of 'the lake in the north' and who or what exactly 'the Ds' were. But there was a problem. Books were expensive (at the time a Ransome would cost 100 times more than a daily paper) and book tokens and valedictory tips from uncles made an irregular appearance. Libraries, in those post-war years, were badly stocked. So I had to beg, borrow or, failing that (kick-starting an enjoyable habit that has continued to this day), rummage around for battered copies in second-hand junk shops.

A clue to the attraction of the series lies in the title of my first purchase. The author, through his characters, works hard to create a secret, private world that floods the child's mind with surprise and delight. A world where the rules are decided by the children themselves, rather than arbitrary adults. A world in the looking-glass of their imagination. It only requires a sufficient drop in the temperature for the houseboat to become Nansen's 'Fram' and a derelict ruin to be turned into an igloo. The intrusion of the unwanted adult is avoided by scrambling under bridges rather than crossing open roads, or by fleeing home comforts to camp or live in a deserted bothy. Their public communications are coded so that only they can understand. Other people, however, are realistically unavoidable and, as the plot unfolds, the secret and real worlds rub along together comfortably enough, one supplementing and influencing the other. When Ransome does allow adults into the story, he chooses, as the necessary enablers, men and women who are outsiders, who have forsaken the conventions of adult behaviour. Old men home from the sea or tramping the Andes, reluctantly leaving their worlds of tea-clippers and fossicking for ore. They have a freedom of spirit seemingly denied to those who shuffle and order most children's lives. The local adults in the cast have lived for all time, sheep farmers, wherrymen, blacksmiths and charcoal burners tending the fires of their everlasting pitsteads. It was the latter who fired Ransome's clay pipes and left them to be collected at the Red Lion, which was one of the reasons he took this route.

Another short stretch of macadam takes us to Grassgarth, where we leave the road and strike up the hill through a wood and into the parklands of Bigland Hall. A much bigger tarn appears and the view from the top of the rise suggests that, at last, you are about to enter the Lake District proper. Drop again to a valley, this time the course of the river Leven, and only the A590 offers further resistance. Play your cards right and you will cross no more than three traffic-infested roads before you reach Carlisle.

During this approach, we will pass through the hamlet of Haverthwaite and a property called Melody Cottage. This is not a reference to the harmony in which its inhabitants undoubtedly lived, but to a former public house where Ransome would pause and reward himself with a pint of beer for his efforts. The Hark to Melody was one of a string of pubs in the north west of England that bear variations on that name. We have already passed the Hark to Bounty at Slaidburn and, as with many inn names, there is a logical explanation for what appears an enigmatic title. The variation is in the last word: Melody, Bounty, Tranter, Ringer, etc. These are names of a famous leading hound in the local pack. 'Hark to' is a hunting term, a cry used when the pack had lost the scent, meaning 'go to' or 'follow' the dog in question to re-establish the chase.

Once over the autobahn, you have merely to follow quiet back roads to the Red Lion at Lowick Bridge, where you can catch up with Ransome, who by then would have collected his churchwarden and been on his second pint of the day.

But Ransome had reasons other than pipes and pints for visiting the Red Lion. As a young man, while camping on the Coniston Fells, he had struck up an acquaintanceship with the artist and historian, W G Collingwood, who was John Ruskin's biographer and general factotum. Collingwood lived at Lanehead, near the north end of the lake, and once Ransome had plucked up sufficient courage to visit the family, a major influence entered his life. Not only did Collingwood, whose artistic tastes and opinions coincided with Ransome's, quickly become a substitute father figure, but the rest of his family welcomed the young writer with open arms and Lanehead became a refuge where he stayed, wrote and messed about in boats. He was particularly fond of the younger daughter, Barbara, but after two years of havering, she decided that lifelong friendship was the more desired outcome to the relationship.

In fact, it was the older sister, Dora, who unwittingly provided a prize that was arguably just as great. After a lengthy courtship—it appears that the Collingwood ladies were not the sort of girls who rushed into things—she married Ernest Altounyan, a doctor, who took her to Syria. In due course they and their children returned to visit the grandparents at Lanehead. Ransome, who took part enthusiastically in teaching them fishing and sailing and encouraging their exploration of the lake and surrounding shores, was adopted as an honorary uncle. Further visits to Lanehead ensued and on one of these Ransome, now living at Low Ludderburn, received a call from Altounyan saying he and the family were about to pay him a visit. Ransome, who was feeling rather under the weather, did not wish to be plagued by a tribe of children and stressed that Ernest alone was to come. Therefore, when all the family poured out of the car, he met the visitors in anything but a welcoming frame of mind. But any rebuff was pre-empted by a surprise presentation of a magnificent pair of Turkish slippers. It had completely slipped Ransome's mind that it was his birthday. Filled with remorse, he determined to repay their thoughtfulness by writing a story about their adventures on and around the lake. So *Swallows and Amazons*, along with Ransome's reputation, was born.

It is only when you view the books through the prism of literary experience that you see how well written these stories are. Essentially they are accounts of a mission or adventure with some goal in mind. As with all quest stories from *Hamlet* to *A Passage to*

India, the search reveals more about the characters involved than it does about the imagined pot of gold. The stories appear to cover a time span of four years and are populated by children who fall into two distinct age-groups. Each of the older group is at one point or another put through some emotional or moral trial. The younger children are at the stage where they are still watching and learning, becoming slowly aware that they too will have to forsake the self-absorption and private games that are the hallmark of the child and start to accept social responsibilities for their actions.

Although each book can be read as a separate entity, together they form a saga that traces the growing-up of the children over a relatively short period of their actual lifetime. A clever structure whereby the protagonists are split into various groups so that they can have separate but overlapping adventures allows this period to be spread over a dozen books and sixteen publishing years. Continuity is maintained as events and memories of one group spill over into another. In this way, the gathering of the whole clan becomes only necessary at three strategic points. At each, the reader can judge how the characters of the children are developing by the way they interact. In the first, *Winter Holiday*, the decisions are made by the older children, and the younger children for the most part merely join in the action rather than instigate it. In a crisis, their immediate response is to wish their elders were present. In *Pigeon Post*, particular expertise in dowsing and metallurgy, essential to the outcome, is beyond the older group and provided by the younger. In the final volume *Great Northern?* it is the youngest who deal with the unexpected while the captains and mates are given comparatively bit parts. More significantly in that story, the hostility of the adults is real, not semi make-believe as in some of the earlier books. The time has come for them to leave the shell of their childhood and, simultaneously, for the author to lay down his pen.

I am not suggesting that these youthful experiences are presented with the same intensity as the rites of passage described by Wordsworth, Conrad or Joyce, but they draw from the same well. As you would expect in any children's adventure story, the overriding impression is one of a series of escapades and activities that gradually merge towards some high point of drama. These include being trapped in old copper workings, drifting out to sea, getting caught in a blizzard and even being on the run from the Law. Serious injury or death is a real possibility, but any potential melodrama is tempered by the children concentrating on the practicalities of seeking a solution to the problem. For this reason, suspense and interest aroused by the events are kept nicely in balance with credibility. So the reader, as well as being caught up in the drama, learns how to sail, survey unknown territory and master skills that local children regard as a given. The children's enthusiasm for these tasks engages the young reader in equal manner. So much so that the author instructs on a variety of practical and intellectual accomplishments without the slightest hint of pedagogy.

But for me, and I expect many others, the enduring appeal of Ransome's writing is his sense of place. The Lakes and Norfolk Broads are sketched with the most delicate of penstrokes. No purple passages that children usually and understandably skip, but a slow unfolding of detail. This is not only topographical, though the reader is left with a very precise impression of Wild Cat Island and the perils of the Yarmouth bridges, but, more importantly, the feeling of place is given by what has eternally gone on in the localities. As you pass through the series, you meet charcoal burners, copper miners, boatbuilders and river pilots, along with accounts of high mountain climbing, hound trailing and pike fishing. There are locals at hand to explain to the children, and thus the reader, the mysteries of tickling trout, walking on mudflats and babbing for eels.

This sense of place explains why you are now faced with a choice of routes as you leave the Red Lion. The more obvious and easier option is to join the Cumbrian Way at Kiln Bank and cross the moor past Beacon Tarn to Torver. Then follow the lakeside path to the village of Coniston. There is a certain symmetry in this approach to the fells proper, for we will leave them at Caldbeck by the same waymarked path. But for the Ransome enthusiast, there is little choice. The east shore of Coniston is Ransome country. He spent his childhood holidays at Nibthwaite and it is the adjacent fells and streams that were transformed into his imagined world. There seems little doubt to me that it was this area that formed the backdrop to the Lakeland stories and though bits and pieces of Windermere have been dragged across the hill, it is here that the stories, at least emotionally, are set.

Assuming, with me, you take to the east, there is a high road or a low road, of which perhaps the better is to leave the lakeside and work over Bethecar Moor to Top o' Selside. Either way, on this stretch can be found 'Holly Howe', 'The Dog's Home', 'Octopus Lagoon on the Amazon River' and 'Wild Cat Island' with its secret harbour. At the north end of the lake

Lowick Bridge to Coniston

are the workings of 'High Tops' on Wetherlam and the Old Man. The author of this fictitious country has pulled around the actual a bit, shifting the props to suit the set, but the picture of his world was so settled in Ransome's mind that he confessed he was sufficiently confused, when he re-examined the reality, to feel that some titanic force must have rearranged things in the night.

Unlike the rest of your journey through the Lakes, you are not liable to meet many tourists in this secretive spot. Once you have left the moor, you can pass through Grizedale Forest easily enough on bulldozed tracks and, by choosing your moment, drop back to the lakeside road at or near Ruskin's house. The road is then followed past Lanehead and the head of the lake to Coniston village itself.

— 7 —

In one fell swoop
Coniston to Wasdale

Coniston is now primarily a tourist centre, a terminus for those sufficiently adventurous to leave the fleshpots of Ambleside to tick off Hawkshead and Tarn Hows. But that was not always the case. It was once a busy railhead created to facilitate the transportation of slate and minerals to the coast for further treatment and shipment. The chief, or at least the most lucrative loot, was the 500 tons a month of copper ore and there is an interesting connection (at least for me) on another twirl of life's roundabout. One of the principal exploiters was the Macclesfield Copper Company, the property of Charles Roe who, after a variety of enterprises, developed a mining business on quite a large scale. The Coniston venture was relatively small in his scheme of things but a fairly large link in the chain of events that developed the industrial prosperity of this area.

Through the ages man might have scraped from the surface sufficient material to manufacture his necessary implements, but the first real mining enterprise in the area was run by the Company of

Mines Royal, started in 1599 and staffed by Germans brought in from the Austrian Tyrol. As the years passed, the easily-obtained ore from outcropping rock was finally exhausted and further developments became necessary. Tunnels were driven into the hillside to connect with unworked parts of the vein. An enterprise which proved anything but easy. Prior to the use of gunpowder to fracture the surface, fires were lit to heat the rock, which was suddenly cooled with cold water and vinegar. The minute fissures caused by this process allowed simple tools to gain purchase, break up the rock and begin to form the mouth of a tunnel.

Naturally, this was long and arduous work and no more rock was cut away than was strictly necessary. As a result, the cross section of the tunnel was ominously coffin-shaped, four foot six inches high and carved in such a way that it was only sufficiently wide at the top to accommodate the head, then gradually tapering from the shoulders to the floor. These tunnels, in turn, produced more problems, as water naturally permeated from above and had to be pumped out before the day's work could begin. Eventually a drain or adit had to be driven in at the lowest level possible, which could run for miles and take up all the water from the workings above. At times, the miners used to try to stem the flow from one working to another by inserting false floors made of clay, supported by timber bracing. These, by now, are extremely vulnerable and one of several reasons why it is *very* dangerous to venture into the mines without the guidance of an expert.

A result of all this activity is that the hillside must be riddled hollow with tunnels and echoing caverns now long forgotten. It is little wonder the miners told of 'knockers', mysterious beings who produced the inexplicable sounds of men at work on long-abandoned seams. It may all be part of a superstitious past but, along with a ban on whistling, they deemed it prudent to leave a few crumbs from their bait-box for the little people. Our route north wends its way amongst the remnants of this now defunct industry and it is here we bid farewell to the creator of *Swallows and Amazons*, for this is the northern edge of Ransome country, the setting for perhaps his most successful story, *Pigeon Post*.

'Old Man' is a term used to describe a worked-out mine and the hill is most certainly that. But the more likely explanation is that it is a hierarchical term to denote prominence, for in other parts of the North, terms like Lads Hill and Little Man are often given to lower eminences.

When you eventually reach the summit, you are standing on what was the highest point in Lancashire. Now it heads no list. It is not even in the top ten of Lakeland Marilyns. What with the Yorkie usurper, the Red Rose does not seem to have been given much of a deal. Perhaps it was seen by some as payback time for the Battle of Bosworth. The Old Man deserves better, for it is the highest point of an arm that embraces the corrie of Goat's Water and the splendid Dow Crag and gives the first real indication of things to come.

This view heralds one of the greatest attractions of this district, the juxtaposition of mountainside and water, and amongst the best is a variety of tarns nestling amongst eroding walls of rock. And their fascination is not limited to the aesthetic. One November morning in 1959, Colin Dodgson and Timothy Tyson, both of Grasmere, reached the bank of just such a tarn, protecting their exposed flesh as best they could against a barrage of hail. Their exposure was somewhat greater than that experienced by the average fell walker. No anoraks or overtrousers for this pair as they climbed out of what was the culmination of a list. In their estimation there were 463 large and small tarns in the Lake District and they had just completed their 463rd early morning dip.

Why, in all weathers, they chose to submit their flesh to this particular form of mortification is hard to imagine. Undoubtedly, lists had something to do with it. Dodgson had completed all the Munros in 1951 and was sixteenth on the all-time list. More significantly, he had also completed what was then the 543 separate mountains and their tops, rather than the more modest ambition of separate mountains alone. He had also climbed all the 3,000ers 'furth of Scotland' and all the tops over 2,000 feet in England and over 2,500 in Wales. Tyson, aged 76, had not started compiling until he was in his fifties but was hard on his heels. So lists may have been a part of it, but the *Manchester Guardian* correspondent Harry Griffin was probably closer to the mark when he suggested that a deeper-seated reason was to discover and understand, as completely as possible, the land in which they lived and worked.

Once on the top you are, again, faced with a choice. In fact, the beauty of a place like the Lakes is that there is always a choice. No barbed wire and deliberately derelict stiles. Nor a place where the landowners are hostile, the farmers curmudgeonly or the sportsmen welcoming with friendly fire. This being the case, it is possible to reach Threlkeld in one determined step or indulge in detours en route. Unless your visit to

Coniston to Wasdale Head

ELL△ Michleden...

Crinkle Crags

Three
Shire
Stone.

Wrynose Pass

SWIRL
HOW △

CONISTON
◎

△
THE OLD MAN
OF CONISTON

G.R.Dale
Mar '08.

the hills is on a par with a pilgrimage to the Adonis Fitness Club, there is no real choice. But given that some budding Narcissus might, whilst searching for a suitable warm-up exercise, peruse these pages, I will outline an option.

Many years ago, I planned and executed a walk/trot to raise money for my school's rugby tour to the Antipodes. My aim was to travel from the top of Coniston Old Man to the top of Skiddaw, losing as little height as possible and visiting twenty-five separate fells (one for every year I had taught there) en route. It took a relatively fit fifty year-old around sixteen hours, including a couple of breaks. I suspect, if you stopped at Threlkeld, where there is accommodation and refreshment available, you could knock an hour off that. The best of the route is that there are only two real descents and ascents. The first is into Wrynose Pass, the second to Dunmail Raise between Steel Fell and Helvellyn. Even these low points are relatively high and the total loss of height between them is less than 3,000 feet. There are, of course, other ups and downs but of such a gradient that each is a change rather than a chore. For the record, the route travels north along the ridge to Great and Little Carrs, drops into Wrynose Pass, then climbs up the straightforward path until it reaches the col above Langdale, then over Crinkle Crags and Bowfell to Esk Hause. At this point we will have to detour to Scafell Pike to collect the highest point in what was once Cumberland, is now Cumbria and was always England. From Esk Hause, aim for High Raise via Rossett Pike, then descend to Dunmail from Steel Fell. (I threw in a few superfluous Langdale Pikes to make up my numbers.) From the pass, climb to Grisedale Tarn and reach Helvellyn, the highest point in Westmorland, via Dollywagon Pike. Then, a quick scamper over the Dods and down to Threlkeld. As the only two points you *have* to visit are Scafell and Helvellyn, a close scrutiny of the map would probably suggest a few short cuts and a time of twelve hours would be by no means impossible if you walked determinedly uphill and trotted the downhill and flat.

But you would probably feel that to rip through this, the most beautiful part of the North, is a sin and prefer to break the journey into parts. If so, I would, on reaching the summit of Scafell Pike, pause and consider. The best I can suggest is that instead of continuing north, you drop down onto Mickledore and thence to Wasdale, where you can stay at the Wasdale Head Hotel. This will offer the bonus of having a look at Scafell itself, fifty feet lower than its

Pike but in every other respect its superior. The most obvious feature is the rampart of cliffs that guards its north and east approaches, and the most obvious consequence of this is the difficulty of a direct traverse from one Scafell to the other. There is a relatively easy way, as the poet Coleridge discovered. But Broad Stand, as the weakness is called, is not for the fainthearted. It is classed as a rock climb and although by those standards it is relatively straightforward, it is highly polished and any slip would have serious consequences. Suffice to say that a number of fell walkers have been seriously injured in an attempt. The summit can be easily reached by a detour but it is probably more worthwhile to spend that time admiring the view.

For you are now at the birthplace of climbing bits of rock unnecessarily. All summits of the hills south of the Border can be reached without adopting simian tactics to any real degree, but those whose playgrounds were the Alps found that, if you suspended the belief that there was a more straightforward way to the top, off-peak training could take place in the Lakes. Inevitably, what had been first sought as an alternative became a reality and the Great Gullies and Somebody or Other's Chimney were seen as of the same order, if not of the same magnitude, as the

Grépon or the Grandes Jorasses. Notes were taken and guidebooks written, and what local shepherds had for centuries seen as inconvenient obstacles of rock became elevated to a pastime and its record of achievement was incarcerated in the Bodleian and other such worthy institutions. This recreational sport, or sporting recreation, went through a variety of stages from when W P Haskett Smith fought manfully with the innards of Deep Ghyll to this very moment. But between 1880 and 1945 progress may be regarded as falling into three main periods: the Gully and Chimney Period, the Rib and Arête Period and the Slab and Wall Period. After that, it was no, or on some occasions all, holds barred. The first period is without doubt the manful grappling phase and by this method many an obstacle was severely smote. In fact, by 1905, all the obvious smoteables had been manfully so grappled, and matters ground to a halt.

Scafell also featured significantly in the second period, through the efforts of O G Jones, and then into the third through the vision and skill of Siegfried Herford. Both of these were exceptional exponents and the Pinnacle Direct from Lord's Rake and Central Buttress, which, in turn, tackled the 'last great problem of the time', only fell because of their skill and ambition. Lesser mortals felt humble and after Jones' death only six routes were discovered and completed before Herford took up the challenge. Herford's death in 1916 caused an even greater vacuum. Eventually, after the First World War, routes began to reappear on a regular basis but the focus had moved to Snowdonia and the inviolable cliff of Clogwyn d'ur Arddu. The loitering heirs have, for the most part, departed to sunnier climes or to climbing wall mock-ups of Scafell's Great Flake pitch on the once 'most difficult climb in the world'. After all, a chap in lycra finds it hard to rise to the occasion when the temperature hovers around zero and the rock is slimy.

Suitably thoughtful of the feats of our forebears, you can descend Hollow Stones to Wasdale and, provided you've booked a room, a night in the Wasdale Head Inn. Although the club was founded in the Sun Hotel in Coniston, this was the traditional HQ of the Fell & Rock Climbing Club. Thankfully it has not been totally changed. The billiard room, which featured a variety of gymnastic displays and a variation of billiards that would have severely tested Walter Lindrum, has gone, but much of the original survives. It was at the cutting edge of its time and, with the Stable Door Traverse, it even foreshadowed modern climbing habits. It is also extremely well placed. In fact, I would maintain that there is no hotel in Britain that competes with the view and offers such easy access to a variety of fells and crags. No doubt the admirers of the Pen y Gwryd and the King's House in Glencoe would want their say, but the great beauty of opinion is that it is subjective and, as with most first loves, the determination to defend outweighs other judgements. You look up the valley until the light fades, a signal to retire to the bar and plan tomorrow's route.

An interlude
which could turn out to be a rocky road
Wasdale to Langdale

To start my planned digression, you leave the Wasdale Head Inn by the back door and set off to gain the south-west arm of the Mosedale Horseshoe. Possibly the best way is by climbing to Dore Head, then along the ridge via Red Pike to the top of Steeple. From there, descend into Wind Gap before completing the circuit. There is a shorter way to the Gap by following the valley of Mosedale and ascending direct to the pass. This would save a bit of ascent and descent, but I wouldn't recommend it. I have no doubt that the view is biased and I have to admit it is based on my only ascent of this steep incline. It was on the final leg of a rather fraught crossing of northern England, based on Wainwright's Coast to Coast Walk. During the previous week, the upper and sole of my left boot had suddenly parted company and, as I did not want to wear in a new pair during a continuous week's walking, I had the two parts temporarily glued together. Prior to the boot bursting, it had been decided we could manage the thirty miles from Robin Hood's Bay to Osmotherly in one go, thus allowing more interesting diversions when reaching the Lakes.

Unfortunately, the temporary repair had subtly altered the shape of the boot and I was, as it were, starting from scratch. I had no alternative but to knock it into shape en route, but quickly discovered this meant the foot rather than the boot. It was not a happy experience and I had to hobble along for the next couple of days aided by trainers and a variety of anaesthetics. By the time we reached Wasdale, the pain had subsided below the clenched teeth level. I had also decided at this stage that alcohol scored better than paracetamol in the pain-relieving stakes. As this was the last night of our journey and tomorrow to St Bees Head was more or less downhill, a small celebration was in order. My companion pleaded toothache or somesuch excuse and I was left with a group of locals and, on the bar, a barrel that dispensed Theakston's ale directly into the glass. My new-found friends were only too happy to sustain my enthusiasm, for the longer that I, a resident, kept drinking, the more obliged the landlord was to keep serving. A veil should be drawn over my next morning's efforts on the seemingly vertical, sun-baked slopes. Suffice to say that this was one of the brewery's stronger concoctions and that I, too, felt old and peculiar.

I am sure that I am writing for a more wholesome audience and, whichever way is chosen, they will find it but a step from the gap to the summit of Pillar Fell. You can continue the switchback over Kirk Fell and Great Gable to reach Styhead, but I would like to suggest an alternative and that is a high-level traverse that works its way across the side of the fells. By dropping, not too literally, off Pillar's north-facing slope, you will quickly come across one of the Lakes' remoter treasures, Pillar Rock. This more than fulfilled the needs of the homecoming Alpinist, deprived of his beloved Aiguilles, as there was no easy way to the summit. It had already gained a fearsome reputation before its first ascent in 1826. The Tourist Information Manuals of the day were hardly encouraging—'Frightful would be the vision to the timid or those unaccustomed to sights like these'—and Wordsworth consigned it to literary immortality in 1800 with the publication of his poem 'The Brothers'. Curiously enough, after these earliest explorations, matters again quickly ground to a halt. The reason was simple. There were no real targets for the then standard of manful strivings, as Walker's Gully was too hard and Savage Gully wasn't really a gully at all when it approached the critical section.

In due and proper course, the ascent of Walker's Gully proved the apotheosis of the grip'n'pull period. At the very end of the nineteenth century, O G Jones and George Abraham, Keswick photographer, mountain writer and general entrepreneur, were ensconced in the Wastwater Hotel, as it was called at the time, determined to launch an attack on the problem that had defeated all others. The weather was foul and the rest of the climbing guests had thrown in the towel, but the pair hung on, hoping matters might improve. Eventually they were joined by A E Field and, with the support of a reliable third man, decided 'regardless of bad weather and personal discomfort' to give it a go. The gully is in eleven pitches and divided by a series of large chockstones that over the years had become wedged in the fissure. In the conditions, this meant a series of ice-cold waterfalls interspersed with the odd mud avalanche. The quotations are from Abraham's later account of that miserable January day.

At the beginning they tried to avoid the worst of the deluge, but eventually had no option and 'as our ablutions seemed likely to be very thorough', they solemnly consumed their lunch before taking any further action. The hallmark of the writing at this period was a tendency to the laconic and all difficulties

Wasdale Head to Dungeon Ghyll

Tarn

ngleTarn

HIGH RAISE

THUNACAR
KNOTT

ROSSETT
PIKE

PAVEY
ARK

Stickle Tarn

ODG

G.R.Dale
Mar'08

were described with little trace of hyperbole. At one stage, Jones struggled to get through a small gap, so to solve the problem, he emptied his pockets and donated his jacket for Field to sit upon. This luxury was not long lived before the third man was called into the fray and, with this additional support, they were 'able to force the leader through the hole amid the sound of tearing clothes and muffled remonstrances from their owner'.

Eventually, they reached the final pitch which had to date repelled all comers. It began to sleet heavily and 'a sudden seriousness settled on all of us'. After an initial fruitless struggle, Jones once more removed his coat and, to maximise the utility of the rugosities on the adjoining rock wall, dispensed with his boots. Much manful struggling later, a torrent of snow and a triumphant *jödel* announced his success. The others followed, thankful for the support of the rope. However, 'one little excitement was still in store'. Jones informed them he probably had frostbite in his toes, which turned out upon examination to be the case. The problem was solved in the (unspecified) 'usual manner' and by placing his feet in 'the pockets of the warmest member of the party'. No doubt, despite being soaked to the skin and on the verge of hypothermia, they scampered back to Wasdale with the enthusiasm of that chap who travelled post-haste from Aix to Ghent. Of course, purists might query whether, as at certain points Jones' toes probably froze onto the rock, this ascent could be classified as totally unaided.

Our high-level traverse first reaches the pass of Black Sail, then, after crossing Kirk Fell on a similar contour, circumnavigates Great Gable by the Climbers' Traverse, so named because it passes under the Napes ridges which were ideally constructed to represent the second, or Rib and Arête Period, of Lake District climbing. If not the most famous, the most historically interesting of these is Eagle's Nest Direct, climbed in 1892 by the future Mayor of Birkenhead, G A Solly, ably aided and abetted by W C Slingsby. This was a remarkable *tour de force* for, in recent guidebooks, the route is still graded Very Severe, regardless of the present advantage of fancy footwear and modern belaying devices. Almost needless to say, it was also completed on a not particularly pleasant April afternoon. For many years an enlarged photograph of a climber (the same A E Field of Walker's Gully) delicately balanced on the crux adorned the dining room wall of the hotel. It acted as an inspiration to many as they prepared for the day's efforts but, sadly, it has now, looking rather sorry for itself, been relegated to the entrance hall.

But probably the most influential chunk of rock is the obelisk called Napes Needle. It was first noticed by W P Haskett Smith when, across the valley, 'the outer-most curtain of mist seemed to be drawn aside and one of the fitful gleams of sunshine fell on a slender pinnacle of rock ... appearing to shoot up for 200 to 300 feet.' Initial attempts to locate this apparition failed, probably because its actual height was around fifty feet, but eventually he found and climbed it solo in June 1886. It was a daring enterprise, as the summit of the Needle is a seemingly unattached block and a final pull on the top (always assuming a firm grip could be found) could mean dislodgement of block and climber alike. Summoning the blood and feeling 'like a mouse climbing a millstone', he cautiously made his way to its highest point. Here he jammed a handkerchief in a crack before tackling the even more daunting task of the descent. Terra firma, therefore, must have been greeted with a mixture of relief and pride as he momentarily watched his abandoned linen waving in the breeze before returning to base.

Haskett Smith returned fifty years later and reclimbed his Needle to the approval of a large crowd of onlookers. Since the first ascent, the climbing world and its wife (and no doubt several men and theirs dogs) have been up and down the polished piece of rock. One man even stood on his head on the apex and the climb itself is a comfortable fixture in the lower order of current difficulty. But its place in history is assured. The Fell & Rock adopted it as a totem and its outline appears as a logo on their publications. O G Jones is said to have been inspired to take up the sport when he saw a photograph of it in a London shop window and although Haskett Smith climbed mountain ranges all over the world, the Father of British Rock Climbing is chiefly remembered for his bold assault of this 'slender pinnacle'.

If your interest lies more in the romantic version of local history than in odd rock formations, you could alternatively traverse the north and gloomier face of Gable. A path that joins the Climbers' Traverse to Honister Pass is known as Moses Trod and from time immemorial has been shrouded in mystery. This particular Moses is thought, by turn, to have been a smuggler, whisky distiller and dealer in precious metals. The common factor of these activities is that they were all likely to excite the interest of the Law, and the Trod is presumed to be the route that facilitated them. Whether Moses actually existed and was gainfully employed in any of these occupations is open to question. If you wanted to smuggle contraband goods, there must have been easier ways to your market place than dragging it over Great Gable. Even if the remote Wasdale was a good drop-off point, the obvious way out was over Styhead.

As for the whisky manufacture, whilst accepting that an illicit still had to be kept away from prying eyes, it seems a bit extreme to perch it, as tradition has it, several scores of feet up a rock climb on Gable Crag. So the rogue's reputation lies with the most likely option, that he stole, or at least 'fenced', the high quality plumbago mined in Borrowdale, which even in those days fetched £800 a ponyload, then shuttled it over the hill to avoid detection. In all, I feel the most likely explanation is that Moses is a myth, a number of local eccentrics that time has merged into one. Nevertheless, on Moses Trod, when the mist is down and dark is falling fast, it is not difficult to believe that the grey figure that looms before you before disappearing into the gloom is not the more probable lump of rock but some body or other about his evening's business.

Either way, you round Gable and land at Styhead, the great crossroads of the Central and Western Fells. A tarmac road, blasting its way from Wasdale to Borrowdale, was once threatened, but wiser counsels or a lack of funds prevailed. Continue past Tarns Styhead and Sprinkling and over what many people call Esk Hause (the true pass between Eskdale and Borrowdale lies 100 feet above and 300 yards south) until, having passed Angle Tarn and descended Rossett Ghyll, you can saunter down the winding Langdale lanes to the comforts of the Old Dungeon Ghyll Hotel.

— 8 —

Further fun and games
Langdale to Caldbeck

The ODG, for so it is known countrywide, was another of the hotels adopted by the Fell & Rock and used as a base by the academics and professional classes that made up its ranks. It was not as regarded as the Wastwater Hotel, which had easier access to Scafell, Pillar and Gable. Moreover, Langdale, though pleasant enough, did not have the brooding grandeur of Wasdale's 'stanes and watter'. All changed when Sid Cross and his wife Alice took over the hotel in 1949. Cross was a climber and he was also a local working-class man, which gave him a head start in realising the implications of the social changes that had been brought about by the war. He also knew that the new generation of climber typified by the likes of Joe Brown and Don Whillans were not necessarily smitten with the ethos dispensed by Geoffrey Winthrop Young & Co, so he converted an old cowshed into a climbers' bar and encouraged the lads from the inner cities to set up base in the area.

To continue your journey, leave the hotel and climb the thousand or so feet of man-made steps and stairs to a hanging valley that harbours Stickle Tarn. This, in turn, is dominated by Pavey Ark, a great lump of rock that soars 800 feet, a sort of flying buttress to the Langdale Pikes. For thirty years it boasted only a few routes of the traditional gully and chimney variety and even when climbers emerged from the gloom to try their luck on the sunlit faces, it was merely to creep around the edges, avoiding the more obvious challenge. Nevertheless, because this side of the valley is peppered with crags of various sizes and varying difficulties, with a southern aspect and relative ease of access, it quickly became popular with the new breed of climbers. They brought with them fresh skills honed on Pennine gritstone and manufactured new routes that relied more on balance and cunning than brute strength and bulldog spirit. The loftier cliffs of Scafell and Pillar no longer held sway and were left to wrap their neglect in appropriate shrouds of mist.

The epitome of this period was a route climbed on nearby Gimmer Crag by Arthur Dolphin in 1948. He named it Kipling Groove, on the grounds that he had found it 'ruddy 'ard'. This steep and imposing line appeared the culmination of the efforts of those who had been prepared to leave the more secure comforts of chimney-squeezing or arête-straddling, but in reality it was the shape of things to come.

It was much more ambitious in its conception than anything that had gone before and required a psychological edge that had never been previously demanded. Not surprisingly, by the third ascent, a piton had been driven into the rock to protect the crux and, as the '65 guide put it, 'time and fear have hallowed its use'.

Although I am not suggesting anything of that nature for the gentle rambler, it is possible to sharpen the senses and gain a few hundred feet through ascending our next objective by Jack's Rake, which runs diagonally across Pavey Ark, thus saving a flog up a mixture of scree and grass. The Rake is made up of a series of easy rock steps and comfortable ledges and gradually makes its way from bottom right to top left. It is not technically a rock climb, as can be judged by the comments of the ultra-conservative Wainwright who, whilst not fully recommending it, does not, as with his warning on Broad Stand, condemn it out of hand. Nevertheless, it would be wise to err on the side of caution, particularly in poor weather or if accompanied by a female companion called Jill. From the summit, paths lead to High Raise (aka High White Stones) and you rejoin my 'Lakeland Direct' en route. From there to the undistinguished top of Steel Fell is a gentle declination, followed by

THRELKELD.

GREAT DOD

WATSON'S DOD

Red Tarn

HELVELLYN

DOLLYWAGON PIKE

Grisedale Tarn

Dunmail Raise

STEEL FELL

HIGH RAISE

THUNACAR KNOTT

PAVEY ARK

Stickle Tarn

ODG

G.R.Dale
Mar '08

Old Dungeon Ghyll to Threlkeld

anything but, down the knee-jerker to Dunmail Raise.

You leave this point on the A591 by an obvious path to Grisedale Tarn and from there a steeper slope leads to the start of the Helvellyn range. Once you are up, life for the walker is easy. There is no significant drop until you skitter down to Threlkeld, navigation is straightforward and the going is good. It must be one of the easiest big mountains to ascend in the district. When I first started teaching, I was invited to assist the school's mountain course. It was an annual event held during the first week of the summer holidays and based, curiously as it was an all boys establishment, at the YWCA in Ambleside. The course leader, very much of the old school, had swallowed wholemeal the Word as spoken by the Alpine Club and each step was planned with military precision. The public bus disgorged us at Wythburn and the boys were informed to the minute how long it would take to reach the summit cairn. It always did, although to the initiated there was usually a perceptible quickening or slackening of our leader's pace to suit the circumstance. There was a re-counting of heads and after a morally instructive tour of the summit furniture, which included memorials to a faithful hound and the landing of an aeroplane, it was down Swirral Edge, lunch at and a dip in Red Tarn before the highlight of scrambling up Striding and returning to Dunmail Raise via Dollywagon Pike and Grisedale Tarn. The bus was boarded in an orderly fashion and—be ready for tea at 6.30 prompt!

Inevitably, the younger members of staff thought this was a bit tame and that, when the opportunity arose, they would do better. The venue duly moved to a proper Mountaineering Club Hut in North Wales, where a couple of minibuses and self-catering allowed more flexibility. The additional activities now included rock climbing and sea canoeing rather than surveying Angle Tarn and make-believe mountain rescues. But the pedagogue had not entirely disappeared. In the obligatory lesson on Mountain Craft, the boys were solemnly informed that in the event of a mountain storm it was essential to abandon the rock face as soon as possible and that the second quickest way to reach the foot of the crag was by abseil. It didn't take long before some fifteen year-old, to the amusement of his peers, asked the obvious question. Of course, in these days of global travel, the same school now visits mountain ranges the world over and, no doubt, the younger members of staff are regaled with stories concerning the amusing lack of vision of those old boys of the last century. There are probably pros and cons for all these approaches but it seems to me that each is better educational practice than driving the children through a series of tests that seem to achieve little other than justifying often spurious objectives.

But back to the present. You have now visited the highest point in what was Westmorland and the last County Top on this first part of the journey. Seven down, seven to go. Among the virtues of this section is, as already mentioned, the easy going, and it is for that reason that many choose it for the darkest hours of twenty-four hour jaunts such as the Bob Graham Round. First completed in 1932, the ascent of these forty-two separate peaks produces a round of seventy-two miles and 27,000 feet of climbing. Although his achievement stood for twenty-eight years, by the sixties the aura was beginning to fade and people started to add further peaks to the course. In 1972 the legendary fell runner, Joss Naylor upped the ante to seventy-two peaks and the current record, held by Mark Hartell, is seventy-seven, achieved in the allowed diurnal unit.

It began to look as if the only limit was the boundary of the National Park, but one thing was clear. These competitors, for surely that is what they have become, are no longer fell walkers blessed with a good 'engine', but athletes who indulge in a training regime that includes nutritional and psychological advice. What was once a pastime is now a sport. Not that there is anything wrong with sport. In fact Cumbria, over the centuries, has invented and excelled at a number. The nearest to the above is the fell race. This is the sprint as opposed to the marathon, distances being relatively short, but with the number of feet ascended being a significant percentage of the yards covered. The sport is relatively simple in its conception. You run up to the top of the hill, then hurl yourself down to the bottom; the less often your feet touch the ground, the more likely you are to win.

This event in the form of the Guide Race formed part of the ubiquitous local Sports. I have written elsewhere of how, on a family holiday, an ascent of Striding Edge awoke my interest in climbing mountains, but that fortnight spent on the shores of Ullswater produced a variety of delight. The huge papier-mâché relief map of the Lake District which resided on the top floor of the photographers, G P Abraham Ltd, rowing the hotel boat across the lake, the well-equipped games room with table-tennis and a full size billiard table, still fill the mind some sixty years later, but it was the Grasmoor Sports that really widened the eyes of this particular townie. Along with the fell race, there was the Cumberland and

Westmorland wrestling, which proved conclusively that a good littl'un can beat a less skilful big'un, and the sheepdog trial, patiently developing to a climax long after most visitors had gone. But it was the hound trailing that really caught my eye and ear.

I had really no idea what was going on when the hounds were released, until a little later the dragman appeared, pulling his sack of paraffin oil and aniseed over the finishing line. Some further time passed before a sense of anticipation stirred among the betting fraternity and there in the middle distance was a flash of colour amongst the bracken, then as mist suddenly parts to reveal its visual cameo, a single dog sped across a small clearing before the bracken once more closed upon the fleeting vision. It seemed from the comments of those around me that they not only knew what was where, but also the likely winner. Within minutes, a cacophony of whistles, shouts and cheers urged the leaders towards the winning post and then it was all over, the victor receiving some morsel and (that hallmark of the North) a restrained pat of affection. The latecomers dribbled in, tails wagging more in hope than expectation.

You won't have covered the ground from Helvellyn to Threlkeld at hound speed, but you will probably be equally relieved to have reached the finishing line of the Salutation Inn, where you will not be surprised to find that the hounds have beaten you to it. Over the fifty years I have visited the establishment, the walls have been adorned with stuffed foxes and various parts of their anatomy. For we are now entering John Peel country.

Only two legs are left on the journey north and as you will not see the Lakes again other than in the far distance, it is probably best to consider how you are going to spend your last day there. All choices start from Skiddaw House and my preferred is the high level route over Great Calva, Knott and Great Lingy Hill before ascending High Pike, the last outpost of the district.

It is surprising how quickly it all ends. One moment, it is all lakes and mountains, then nothing but fields and woods. The explanation resides at the heart of Carrock Fell over to the east. This was the scene of a massive geological pile-up as various rock types and formations came into collision. Once the mess had sorted itself out, the existing landscape emerged. From here, your next objective, Caldbeck, is straight ahead down the northern slopes through the hamlet of Nether Row. Best to pause a while and bid your farewells. From this side, Blencathra, that imposing bastion which confronts the traveller

161

from the motorway on the road in from Keswick, does not, like so much when viewed from the rear, look at its most impressive. Here, there is none of the graceful skyline and soaring ridges that is its outward appearance, only a gentler common rolling towards the valley bottom. Yet these Northern Fells are an interesting part of the world and though they are now more popular than they were, they still offer a welcome change from the Central and Southern Fells that seem always to teem with folk from south Lancashire and the north Midlands. They might not offer the drama of Wasdale or the glamour of Langdale but there is a rounded charm about them.

However, the charm can wear a bit thin when the weather changes for the worst. This northern salient takes the brunt from the east and has learnt to keep its head down, and in some conditions you would be advised to do the same. In which case, the high ground can be avoided and the shelter of the valley sought by following the wet-weather alternative of the Cumbrian Way, for just below Skiddaw House you have bumped into it again. This works its way north until, clear of the hills, it swings to the east to reconnect at Nether Row. Then again, you may feel that, having conquered the other Lake District giants, you may as well go for a nap hand by ascending

⊙ CALDBECK

Nether Row

• Branthwaite

• Longlands

△ HIGH PIKE   Calebrack

• Orthwaite

△ KNOTT

△ CARROCK FELL

• Peter House Farm

△ COCKUP

△ GREAT CALVA

• Skiddaw House

△ SKIDDAW

△ BLENCATHRA

⊙ THRELKELD

G.R.Dolé.
Mar '08

Threlkeld to Caldbeck

Skiddaw. If so, it's just above you, 2,000 feet above you. Once the summit is ticked off, you continue north until you too reach the edge of all things and can descend to join the Wet Weather at Peter House Farm.

If you decide on the Skiddaw option, it would again be wise to study the map with some care, for you could easily stray onto a protuberance marked Cockup. Strangers to the district might be curious as to the origins of this singular name. Perhaps a further topographical reference might give a clue. In the vicinity is Dead Crag and below that Dead Beck. One foolish mistake at a critical moment and you could find yourself being transported by this particular tributary of the River Styx, within Charon's watery grasp. Support for this etymological interpretation is offered from across the valley. For there stands Great Cockup, surrounded, or so it appears, by a posse of life-threatening grouse butts. As with the Fenwick Arms, you have been warned.

If you decide to break the journey at Caldbeck rather than soldiering on the thirteen miles to Carlisle, an evening stroll to Hesket Newmarket will repay your efforts. The Old Crown is a small village pub with a brewery attached, which concocts an excellent variety of ales, echoing with names such as Skiddaw

Special, Scafell Blonde and of, course, Great Cockup Porter, to restir the memory. As the surrounding area seems to be a bolthole for a number of celebrities (Charles Dickens and Wilkie Collins stayed here) you might even recognise a familiar face or two. The photographs on the wall give a hint.

All this area is known as Back o' Skiddaw and it was around the back of Skiddaw that John Peel made his name. He is probably the most renowned Cumbrian and his final resting place is Caldbeck churchyard, marked by a memorial topped with hound and horns. Unlike many figures of folklore, he was well known in his lifetime and it is reputed that 3,000 people were present at his funeral at St Kentigern's church. In shifting times, locals believed he stood for something that was quintessentially Cumbrian and overlooked his weaknesses to praise his (and their) strengths. Even after death he was not forgotten and in 1954 thousands flocked to the village to attend its centenary celebrations.

It may be that he was universally known but he was not universally admired. In 1929, the Rector of Caldbeck berated his flock that they should 'make a hero of one who has neglected his farm and impoverished his family by his unrestrained pursuit of hunting' and even as good a friend as John

Woodcock Graves admitted that when the cry was on, nothing could stop him, even 'the impending death of a child', and he had thirteen of those. In fact, Peel owes his notoriety to the said Graves who wrote the words of the song that became an overnight Society hit when performed at a charity dinner in London. Today's renditions are often as flawed as the huntsman's character. His coat was 'grey' not 'gay', an assumption based on depictions of The Quorn and its like. There was no hound called 'True'; 'true' was used as a comparative compliment to suggest that the whole pack was as sound as its master. Finally, 'Caldbeck' is often replaced by the more renowned tourist spot, Troutbeck.

Nor does the myth of his singularity in the hunting world bear too close an examination. In the first place, most of his hunting did not take place in the Lake District but in the low country south of Carlisle where, unlike the true Cumbrian huntsman, he chased foxes on horseback rather than on foot. Even in terms of mass slaughter, he was easily outgunned by William Porter of Eskdale. The extent of his celebrity rested on the likes of Sir Wilfrid Lawson and other parvenus enriched by the Industrial Revolution who, having acquired the tithes and titles of the gentry, wanted to take part in their sports. In return for substantial patronage, Peel obliged by introducing them to the cliquish inner circle of the local hunting fraternity.

No doubt, today, John Peel would be a vociferous member of the Countryside Alliance and I am sure that issues and voices would be raised over matters close to his heart. Nor are the arguments as simple as the polemicists would suggest. It is difficult to counter the case for the defence of your own property unless you condemn the majority of activities undertaken by the human race. Farmers don't breed lambs and chickens to ensure foxes maintain a balanced diet. Moreover, you could show, if not sympathy, at least an understanding of the instinctive martial spirit that has sustained human existence and enabled individuals to support themselves and others in moments of crisis. Yet any tolerance should be tempered by circumstance.

The native fox was primarily grey rather than a cuddly russet and this breed was hunted to extinction by the 1880s. The version that peers through the gift shop window was imported from the South for more clear-cut and less defensible reasons. As we have seen, there are a myriad ways to cross the Lakes but whichever way you choose you will see more than one remnant of a fox that was probably as much an off-comer as yourself.

Envoi
Caldbeck to Carlisle

There is a photograph in an early journal produced by the Fell & Rock Climbing Club that shows a view of Pillar Rock from somewhere near Robinson's Cairn. Its outline is softened by mist as if, to borrow a cinematic term, it was about to dissolve into some other image. The title given to the picture is the same as this chapter's, a final rueful glance. Perhaps, oversentimental in its composition, it is, nevertheless, the sort of snapshot that we carry in the wallets of our mind—the train gathering speed as, after leaving the station, it disappears from view. In this case, the nostalgia was understandable since the picture reflected an age when holidays were short and infrequent and travel to the more remote parts of these islands often difficult and expensive. The climber with his back to the camera would probably not see Pillar again for some little time. Another brief encounter.

I certainly experienced a similar feeling on the final stretch of the Cumbrian Way from Caldbeck to Carlisle and the end of the first leg of what I

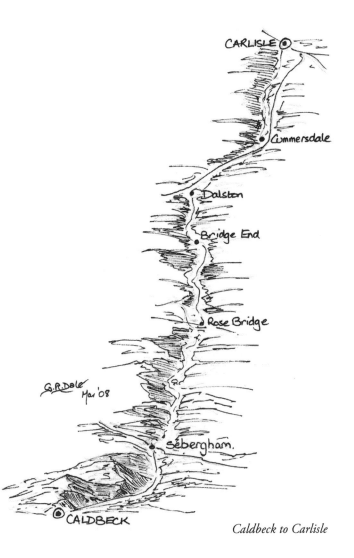

CARLISLE

Cummersdale

Dalston

Bridge End

Rose Bridge

G.R.Dale
Mar '08

Sebergham.

CALDBECK

Caldbeck to Carlisle

have rather grandly thought of as my Great North Circular. From now on, it more or less travels east, then turns south. To reach the city, you simply follow the river Caldew, first met on the flanks of Skiddaw, into virtually the centre, where it suddenly deserts you, swinging away to join the Eden and empty itself into the Solway Firth. Many finish their Cumbrian journey as they come off the Northern Fells, thinking that the interest is effectively over. They may have made a mistake for, like its beginnings, it passes through country rarely visited and often with secrets of its own. The flash of the kingfisher, dippers swimming underwater and weeds that look like Christmas trees that have been ditched to avoid some recycling charge are seen on silent meandering stretches and in sudden lagoons. It even has its own secret valley nestling between the M6 and the main line to Glasgow, just when you're sure that urban life is inevitably about to tumble down upon you.

Even the guidebook is at it, when, as it escorts you to the final high point of the journey, the key shifts from major to minor, inviting the reader to 'take your last lingering look at the Lakeland fells'. The moment reminded me of that photograph and how probably this could be the last long walk I would undertake. But perhaps it is I who am getting unnecessarily sentimental. There's plenty ahead. A quick skip along the ramparts of a long-established Italian construction company allows you to enter what many of my acquaintance consider to be God's own country and strike out for Muckle Cheviot, the most northerly County Top in northern England.

Appendix
Route finders

As already mentioned, the suggested itinerary is just that, and there is no doubt that the same outcome could be achieved in a variety of ways. Nevertheless, I have listed below the publications that I found useful in my planning. These, with the plethora of guidebooks, some of which I have included in the bibliography, should prove more than sufficient to cover most of the ground and, indeed, suggest alternatives or interesting off-track excursions.

In addition, most of the high ground is more than adequately covered by the maps of the OS Outdoor Leisure series which, being often double-sided, cross great tracts of ground. Not so good for wet, windy days, but excellent at the planning stage. The bits and bobs that are left are covered by the Survey's standard model at either at 1:25 000 or 1:50 000. Unfortunately, as already mentioned, the OS has the heel of Achilles. The hills and vales may remain more or less immutable, but town planning is built on all too shifting sand. Fortunately, in this volume, there are only three of these deserts, Littleborough, Burnley and Carnforth. If you want direction with any or all of these, I am happy to provide, on request to the publishers, a pamphlet showing the relevant detail.

Various Ways
The Long Distance Walkers' Handbook, published by A & C Black in 1980 and revised on a regular basis, is of great assistance with any form of long distance walking, as it is a directory of all such routes in the UK and provides information concerning maps required and available relevant publications.

The following (given current availability) may be of use when planning the route from Three Shire Head to Carlisle:

Pennine Way, Edward de la Billiere and Keith Carter, Trailblazer Publications, ISBN 1 873756 57 7

The Peakland Way, John Merrill, JNM Publication, ISBN 0 907496 84 9

Rossendale Way, published by Rossendale Borough Council, c/o Tourist Information Centre, Kay Street, Rawtenstall BB4 7LZ

Pendle Way, Paul Hannon, Hillside Publications, ISBN 1 870141 57 1

Witches' Way, Private publication. Contact David Johnson, c/o Hillside Publications, 12 Broadlands, Keighley BD20 6HX

The North Bowland Traverse, David Johnson,
   Hillside Publications, ISBN 1 870141 01 6

The Cistercian Way, published by the Borough of
   Barrow in Furness, Tourist Information Centre,
   Forum 28, Duke Street, Barrow in Furness
   LA14 1HU

The Cumbria Coastal Way, Roger Cartwright, South
   Lakeland District Council, Leisure Services Dept,
   South Lakeland House, Lowther Street, Kendal
   LA9 4UF

Furness Way, Paul Hannon, Hillside Publications,
   ISBN 1 870141 27 X

The Cumbria Way, Jim Watson, Cicerone Press,
   ISBN 1 85284 242 3

Crossing Morecambe Bay: Galloway's Society for the
Blind (www.galloways.org.uk) organise charity walks
across the bay on a regular basis.

Bibliography

Bates, J: *Rambles Twixt Pendle and Holme* (nd)

Benson, C E: *Crag and Hound in Lakeland* (Hurst & Blackett, 1902)

Bibby, A: *Forest of Bowland* (Frances Lincoln, 2005)

Byne, E and Sutton, G: *High Peak* (Secker & Warburg, 1966)

Dawson, A: *The Relative Hills of Britain* (Cicerone Press, 1992)

Dixon, J: *Historic Walks around the Pendle Way* (Aussteiger Publications, 1990)

Dodd, A E and E M: *Peakland Roads and Trackways* (Landmark Publishing, 2000)

Evans, B: *Walks in Silverdale and Arnside* (Cicerone Press, 1986)

Garnett, E: *The Wray Flood of 1967* (University of Lancaster, 2002)

Gillham, J: *Bowland & The South Pennines* (Grey Stone Books, 1990)

Griffin, A H: *Inside the Real Lakeland* (The Guardian Press, 1961); *In Mountain Lakeland* (The Guardian Press, 1963)

Hadfield, C: *British Canals. An Illustrated History* (David & Charles, 1950)

Hadfield, C & Biddle, G: *The Canals of North West England* Vol 1(David & Charles, 1970); *The Canals of North West England* Vol 2 (David & Charles, 1970)

Hill, H: *Freedom to Roam* (Moorland Publishing, 1980)

Holland, E G: *Coniston Copper Mines* (Cicerone Press, 1981)

Kendall-Price, C: *In the Footsteps of the Swallows and Amazons* (Wild Cat Publishing, 1993)

Lancaster Group of the Ramblers' Association: *Walks in the Lune Valley* (Stramongate Press, 1993)

Lumby, J: *The Lancashire Witch Craze* (Carnegie Publishing, 1995)

Porter, J: *The Making of the Central Pennines* (Moorland Publishing, 1980)

Richards, M: *High Peak Walks* (Cicerone Press, 1982)

Sellers, G: *Walks on the West Pennine Moors* (Cicerone Press, 1979)

Turner, G: *The North Country* (Eyre & Spottiswoode, 1967)

West, J L: *The Taylors of Lancashire* (John L West, 1977)